C000272333

PROMISED DAY IS COME

Written 1941

by Shoghi Effendi:

GOD PASSES BY
THE ADVENT OF DIVINE JUSTICE

Collections of Letters and Messages:

THE WORLD ORDER OF BAHÁ'U'LLÁH
MESSAGES TO THE BAHÁ'Í WORLD
CITADEL OF FAITH
BAHÁ'Í ADMINISTRATION

Translations:

THE KITÁB-I-ÍQÁN
EPISTLE TO THE SON OF THE WOLF
GLEANINGS FROM THE WRITINGS OF BAHÁ'U'LLÁH
PRAYERS AND MEDITATIONS OF BAHÁ'U'LLÁH
THE HIDDEN WORDS

THE
PROMISED
DAY
IS COME

by
Shoghi Effendi

Bahá'í Publishing Trust

WILMETTE, ILLINOIS

Bahá'í Publishing Trust, 415 Linden Ave.,
Wilmette, Illinois 60091

Copyright 1941, © 1969, 1980, 1996 by the
National Spiritual Assembly of the Bahá'ís
of the United States. All rights reserved.
New edition 1980. First pocket-size edition 1996
Printed in the United States of America

15   14   13   12   7   6   5   4

**The Library of Congress has cataloged the
hardcover edition as follows**

Shoghi, Effendi.
        The promised day is come / Shoghi Effendi. —
            1st pocket-size ed.
            p.   cm.
        Includes index.
        ISBN-10: 0-87743-244-9 (Pocket ed.): $8.50
        ISBN-13: 978-0-87743-244-9
        1. Bahai Faith.   I. Title.
BP365.S53 1994
297'.93—dc20

                                                94-37860
                                                     CIP

Cover design by Patrick Falso

PREFACE

[Shoghi Effendi, great-grandson of Bahá'u'lláh, founder of the Bahá'í Faith, was the spiritual head of the Bahá'í World Community from 1921 until his passing in 1957. The following commentary on the origin and aims of the Bahá'í Faith is excerpted from a statement prepared by him in 1947 for the United Nations Special Palestine Committee.]

The fundamental principle enunciated by Bahá'-
u'lláh . . . is that religious truth is not absolute but
relative, that Divine Revelation is a continuous and
progressive process, that all the great religions of the
world are divine in origin, that their basic principles
are in complete harmony, that their aims and purposes
are one and the same, that their teachings are but fac-
ets of one truth, that their functions are complemen-
tary, that they differ only in the nonessential aspects
of their doctrines, and that their missions represent
successive stages in the spiritual evolution of human
society. . . .

    . . . His mission is to proclaim that the ages of
the infancy and of the childhood of the human race
are past, that the convulsions associated with the
present stage of its adolescence are slowly and pain-

fully preparing it to attain the stage of manhood, and are heralding the approach of that Age of Ages when swords will be beaten into plowshares, when the Kingdom promised by Jesus Christ will have been established, and the peace of the planet definitely and permanently ensured. Nor does Bahá'u'lláh claim finality for His own Revelation, but rather stipulates that a fuller measure of the truth He has been commissioned by the Almighty to vouchsafe to humanity, at so critical a juncture in its fortunes, must needs be disclosed at future stages in the constant and limitless evolution of mankind.

iii   The Bahá'í Faith upholds the unity of God, recognizes the unity of His Prophets, and inculcates the principle of the oneness and wholeness of the entire human race. It proclaims the necessity and the inevitability of the unification of mankind, asserts that it is gradually approaching, and claims that nothing short of the transmuting spirit of God, working through His chosen Mouthpiece in this day, can ultimately succeed in bringing it about. It, moreover, enjoins upon its followers the primary duty of an unfettered search after truth, condemns all manner of prejudice and superstition, declares the purpose of religion to be the promotion of amity and concord, proclaims its essential harmony with science, and recognizes it as the foremost agency for the pacification and the orderly progress of human society. . . .

iv   Mírzá Ḥusayn-'Alí, surnamed Bahá'u'lláh (the Glory of God), a native of Mázindarán, Whose advent the Báb [Herald and Forerunner of Bahá'u'lláh] had foretold, . . . was imprisoned in Ṭihrán, was banished, in 1852, from His native land to Baghdád, and thence to Constantinople and Adrianople, and finally to the prison city of 'Akká, where He remained incarcerated for no less than twenty-four years, and in whose neighborhood He passed away in 1892. In the course of His banishment, and particularly in Adrianople and 'Akká, He formulated the laws and ordinances of His Dispensation, expounded, in over a hundred volumes, the principles of His Faith, proclaimed His Message to the kings and rulers of both the East and the West, both Christian and Muslim, addressed the Pope, the Caliph of Islám, the Chief Magistrates of the Republics of the American continent, the entire Christian sacerdotal order, the leaders of Shí'ih and Sunní Islám, and the high priests of the Zoroastrian religion. In these writings He proclaimed His Revelation, summoned those whom He addressed to heed His call and espouse His Faith, warned them of the consequences of their refusal, and denounced, in some cases, their arrogance and tyranny. . . .

The Faith which this order serves, safeguards and promotes is . . . essentially supernatural, supranational, entirely non-political, non-partisan, and diametrically opposed to any policy or school of thought that seeks to exalt any particular race, class or nation. It is free from any form of ecclesiasticism, has neither priesthood nor rituals, and is supported exclusively by voluntary contributions made by its avowed ad-

v

herents. Though loyal to their respective governments, though imbued with the love of their own country, and anxious to promote at all times, its best interests, the followers of the Bahá'í Faith, nevertheless, viewing mankind as one entity, and profoundly attached to its vital interests, will not hesitate to subordinate every particular interest, be it personal, regional or national, to the over-riding interests of the generality of mankind, knowing full well that in a world of interdependent peoples and nations the advantage of the part is best to be reached by the advantage of the whole, and that no lasting result can be achieved by any of the component parts if the general interests of the entity itself are neglected. . . .

—Shoghi Effendi

THE
PROMISED
DAY
IS COME

THE PROMISED DAY IS COME

Friends and fellow-heirs of the Kingdom of Bahá'u'lláh: 1

A tempest, unprecedented in its violence, unpredict- 2
able in its course, catastrophic in its immediate effects,
unimaginably glorious in its ultimate consequences, is
at present sweeping the face of the earth. Its driving
power is remorselessly gaining in range and momentum. Its cleansing force, however much undetected, is
increasing with every passing day. Humanity, gripped
in the clutches of its devastating power, is smitten by
the evidences of its resistless fury. It can neither perceive its origin, nor probe its significance, nor discern
its outcome. Bewildered, agonized and helpless, it
watches this great and mighty wind of God invading
the remotest and fairest regions of the earth, rocking
its foundations, deranging its equilibrium, sundering
its nations, disrupting the homes of its peoples, wast-
ing its cities, driving into exile its kings, pulling down
its bulwarks, uprooting its institutions, dimming its
light, and harrowing up the souls of its inhabitants.

3   *"The time for the destruction of the world and its people,"* Bahá'u'lláh's prophetic pen has proclaimed, *"hath arrived." "The hour is approaching,"* He specifically affirms, *"when the most great convulsion will have appeared." "The promised day is come, the day when tormenting trials will have surged above your heads, and beneath your feet, saying: 'Taste ye what your hands have wrought!'" "Soon shall the blasts of His chastisement beat upon you, and the dust of hell enshroud you."* And again: *"And when the appointed hour is come, there shall suddenly appear that which shall cause the limbs of mankind to quake." "The day is approaching when its* [civilization's] *flame will devour the cities, when the Tongue of Grandeur will proclaim: 'The Kingdom is God's, the Almighty, the All-Praised!'" "The day will soon come,"* He, referring to the foolish ones of the earth, has written, *"whereon they will cry out for help and receive no answer." "The day is approaching,"* He moreover has prophesied, *"when the wrathful anger of the Almighty will have taken hold of them. He, verily, is the Omnipotent, the All-Subduing, the Most Powerful. He shall cleanse the earth from the defilement of their corruption, and shall give it for an heritage unto such of His servants as are nigh unto Him."*

4   *"As to those who deny Him Who is the Sublime Gate of God,"* the Báb, for His part, has affirmed in the Qayyúm-i-Asmá', *"for them We have prepared, as justly decreed by God, a sore torment. And He, God, is the Mighty, the Wise."* And further, *"O peoples of the earth!*

I swear by your Lord! Ye shall act as former generations have acted. Warn ye, then, yourselves of the terrible, the most grievous vengeance of God. For God is, verily, potent over all things." And again: *"By My glory! I will make the infidels to taste, with the hands of My power, retributions unknown of anyone except Me, and will waft over the faithful those musk-scented breaths which I have nursed in the midmost heart of My throne."*

Dear friends! The powerful operations of this ti- 5
tanic upheaval are comprehensible to none except such as have recognized the claims of both Bahá'u'lláh and the Báb. Their followers know full well whence it comes, and what it will ultimately lead to. Though ignorant of how far it will reach, they clearly recognize its genesis, are aware of its direction, acknowledge its necessity, observe confidently its mysterious processes, ardently pray for the mitigation of its severity, intelligently labor to assuage its fury, and anticipate, with undimmed vision, the consummation of the fears and the hopes it must necessarily engender.

This Judgment of God

This judgment of God, as viewed by those who have 6
recognized Bahá'u'lláh as His Mouthpiece and His greatest Messenger on earth, is both a retributory calamity and an act of holy and supreme discipline. It is at once a visitation from God and a cleansing process

for all mankind. Its fires punish the perversity of the human race, and weld its component parts into one organic, indivisible, world-embracing community. Mankind, in these fateful years, which at once signalize the passing of the first century of the Bahá'í Era and proclaim the opening of a new one, is, as ordained by Him Who is both the Judge and the Redeemer of the human race, being simultaneously called upon to give account of its past actions, and is being purged and prepared for its future mission. It can neither escape the responsibilities of the past, nor shirk those of the future. God, the Vigilant, the Just, the Loving, the All-Wise Ordainer, can, in this supreme Dispensation, neither allow the sins of an unregenerate humanity, whether of omission or of commission, to go unpunished, nor will He be willing to abandon His children to their fate, and refuse them that culminating and blissful stage in their long, their slow and painful evolution throughout the ages, which is at once their inalienable right and their true destiny.

"Bestir yourselves, O people," is, on the one hand, the ominous warning sounded by Bahá'u'lláh Himself, *"in anticipation of the days of Divine Justice, for the promised hour is now come." "Abandon that which ye possess, and seize that which God, Who layeth low the necks of men, hath brought. Know ye of a certainty that if ye turn not back from that which ye have committed, chastisement will overtake you on every side, and ye shall behold things more grievous than that which ye beheld*

aforetime." And again: *"We have fixed a time for you, O people! If ye fail, at the appointed hour, to turn towards God, He, verily, will lay violent hold on you, and will cause grievous afflictions to assail you from every direction. How severe indeed is the chastisement with which your Lord will then chastise you!"* And again: *"God assuredly dominateth the lives of them that wronged Us, and is well aware of their doings. He will most certainly lay hold on them for their sins. He, verily, is the fiercest of Avengers."* And finally: *"O ye peoples of the world! Know verily that an unforeseen calamity is following you and that grievous retribution awaiteth you. Think not the deeds ye have committed have been blotted from My sight. By My Beauty! All your doings hath My pen graven with open characters upon tablets of chrysolite."*

"The whole earth," Bahá'u'lláh, on the other hand, forecasting the bright future in store for a world now wrapt in darkness, emphatically asserts, *"is now in a state of pregnancy. The day is approaching when it will have yielded its noblest fruits, when from it will have sprung forth the loftiest trees, the most enchanting blossoms, the most heavenly blessings."* *"The time is approaching when every created thing will have cast its burden. Glorified be God Who hath vouchsafed this grace that encompasseth all things, whether seen or unseen!"* *"These great oppressions,"* He, moreover, foreshadowing humanity's golden age, has written, *"are preparing it for the advent of the Most Great Justice."* This Most Great Justice is indeed the Justice upon which the structure

of the Most Great Peace can alone, and must eventually, rest, while the Most Great Peace will, in turn, usher in that Most Great, that World Civilization which shall remain forever associated with Him Who beareth the Most Great Name.

9   Beloved friends! Well nigh a hundred years have elapsed since the Revelation of Bahá'u'lláh dawned upon the world—a Revelation, the nature of which, as affirmed by Himself, *"none among the Manifestations of old, except to a prescribed degree, hath ever completely apprehended."* For a whole century God has respited mankind, that it might acknowledge the Founder of such a Revelation, espouse His Cause, proclaim His greatness, and establish His Order. In a hundred volumes, the repositories of priceless precepts, mighty laws, unique principles, impassioned exhortations, reiterated warnings, amazing prophecies, sublime invocations, and weighty commentaries, the Bearer of such a Message has proclaimed, as no Prophet before Him has done, the Mission with which God had entrusted Him. To emperors, kings, princes and potentates, to rulers, governments, clergy and peoples, whether of the East or of the West, whether Christian, Jew, Muslim, or Zoroastrian, He addressed, for well-nigh fifty years, and in the most tragic circumstances, these priceless pearls of knowledge and wisdom that lay hid within the ocean of His matchless utterance. Forsaking fame and fortune, accepting imprisonment and exile, careless of ostracism and obloquy, submitting to physical

indignities and cruel deprivations, He, the Vicegerent of God on earth, suffered Himself to be banished from place to place and from country to country, till at length He, in the Most Great Prison, offered up His martyred son as a ransom for the redemption and unification of all mankind. *"We verily,"* He Himself has testified, *"have not fallen short of Our duty to exhort men, and to deliver that whereunto I was bidden by God, the Almighty, the All-Praised. Had they hearkened unto Me, they would have beheld the earth another earth."* And again: *"Is there any excuse left for anyone in this Revelation? No, by God, the Lord of the Mighty Throne! My signs have encompassed the earth, and My power enveloped all mankind, and yet the people are wrapped in a strange sleep!"*

What Response to His Call?

How—we may well ask ourselves—has the world, the object of such Divine solicitude, repaid Him Who sacrificed His all for its sake? What manner of welcome did it accord Him, and what response did His call evoke? A clamor, unparalleled in the history of Shí'ih Islám, greeted, in the land of its birth, the infant light of the Faith, in the midst of a people notorious for its crass ignorance, its fierce fanaticism, its barbaric cruelty, its ingrained prejudices, and the unlimited sway held over the masses by a firmly entrenched ecclesiastical hierarchy. A persecution, kindling a courage which, as attested by no less eminent an authority than the late Lord Curzon of Kedleston, has been unsurpassed by that which the fires of Smithfield evoked, mowed down, with tragic swiftness, no less than twenty thousand of its heroic adherents, who refused to barter their newly born faith for the fleeting honors and security of a mortal life.

11   To the bodily agonies inflicted upon these sufferers, the charges, so unmerited, of Nihilism, occultism, anarchism, eclecticism, immorality, sectarianism, heresy, political partisanship—each conclusively disproved by the tenets of the Faith itself and by the conduct of its followers—were added, swelling thereby the number of those who, unwittingly or maliciously, were injuring its cause.

12   Unmitigated indifference on the part of men of eminence and rank; unrelenting hatred shown by the ecclesiastical dignitaries of the Faith from which it had sprung; the scornful derision of the people among whom it was born; the utter contempt which most of those kings and rulers who had been addressed by its Author manifested towards it; the condemnations pronounced, the threats hurled, and the banishments decreed by those under whose sway it arose and first spread; the distortion to which its principles and laws were subjected by the envious and the malicious, in lands and among peoples far beyond the country of its origin—all these are but the evidences of the treatment meted out by a generation sunk in self-content,

careless of its God, and oblivious of the omens, prophecies, warnings and admonitions revealed by His Messengers.

The blows so heavily dealt the followers of so precious, so glorious, so potent a Faith failed, however, to assuage the animosity that inflamed its persecutors. Nor did the deliberate and mischievous misrepresentations of its fundamental teachings, its aims and purposes, its hopes and aspirations, its institutions and activities, suffice to stay the hand of the oppressor and the calumniator, who sought by every means in their power to abolish its name and extirpate its system. The hand which had struck down so vast a number of its blameless and humble lovers and servants was now raised to deal its Founders the heaviest and cruelest blows.

The Báb— *"the Point,"* as affirmed by Bahá'u'lláh, *"round Whom the realities of the Prophets and Messengers revolve"*—was the One first swept into the maelstrom which engulfed His supporters. Sudden arrest and confinement in the very first year of His short and spectacular career; public affront deliberately inflicted in the presence of the ecclesiastical dignitaries of S͟híráz; strict and prolonged incarceration in the bleak fastnesses of the mountains of Ád͟hirbáyján; a contemptuous disregard and a cowardly jealousy evinced respectively by the Chief Magistrate of the realm and the foremost minister of his government; the carefully staged and farcical interrogatory sustained in the presence of the heir to the Throne and the distinguished divines of Tabríz; the shameful infliction of the bastinado in the prayer house, and at the hands of the <u>Sh</u>ay<u>kh</u>u'l-Islám of that city; and finally suspension in the barrack-square of Tabríz and the discharge of a volley of above seven hundred bullets at His youthful breast under the eyes of a callous multitude of about ten thousand people, culminating in the ignominious exposure of His mangled remains on the edge of the moat without the city gate—these were the progressive stages in the tumultuous and tragic ministry of One Whose age inaugurated the consummation of all ages, and Whose Revelation fulfilled the promise of all Revelations.

15   *"I swear by God!"* the Báb Himself in His Tablet to Muḥammad <u>Sh</u>áh has written, *"Shouldst thou know the things which in the space of these four years have befallen Me at the hands of thy people and thine army, thou wouldst hold thy breath from fear of God. . . . Alas, alas, for the things which have touched Me! . . . I swear by the Most Great Lord! Wert thou to be told in what place I dwell, the first person to have mercy on Me would be thyself. In the heart of a mountain is a fortress* [Mákú] *. . . the inmates of which are confined to two guards and four dogs. Picture, then, My plight. . . . In this mountain I have remained alone, and have come to such a pass that none of those gone before Me have suffered what I have suffered, nor any transgressor endured what I have endured!"*

16   *"How veiled are ye, O My creatures,"* He, speaking with the voice of God, has revealed in the Bayán, *". . .*

who, without any right, have consigned Him unto a mountain [Mákú], *not one of whose inhabitants is worthy of mention. . . . With Him, which is with Me, there is no one except him who is one of the Letters of the Living of My Book. In His presence, which is My Presence, there is not at night even a lighted lamp! And yet, in places* [of worship] *which in varying degrees reach out unto Him, unnumbered lamps are shining! All that is on earth hath been created for Him, and all partake with delight of His benefits, and yet they are so veiled from Him as to refuse Him even a lamp!* "

What of Bahá'u'lláh, the germ of Whose Revela-   17
tion, as attested by the Báb, is endowed with a potency superior to the combined forces of the Bábí Dispensation? Was He not—He for Whom the Báb had
suffered and died in such tragic and miraculous circumstances—made, for nearly half a century and under the domination of the two most powerful potentates of the East, the object of a systematic and concerted conspiracy which, in its effects and duration, is
scarcely paralleled in the annals of previous religions?

"The cruelties inflicted by My oppressors," He Him-   18
self in His anguish has cried out, *"have bowed Me down,
and turned My hair white. Shouldst thou present thyself
before My throne, thou wouldst fail to recognize the Ancient Beauty, for the freshness of His countenance is altered and its brightness hath faded, by reason of the oppression of the infidels. I swear by God! His heart, His
soul, and His vitals are melted!"* *"Wert thou to hear with
Mine ear,"* He also declares, *"thou wouldst hear how 'Alí*

[the Báb] *bewaileth Me in the presence of the Glorious Companion, and how Muḥammad weepeth over Me in the all-highest Horizon, and how the Spirit* [Jesus] *beateth Himself upon the head in the heaven of My decree, by reason of what hath befallen this Wronged One at the hands of every impious sinner.*" "*Before Me,*" He elsewhere has written, "*riseth up the Serpent of wrath with jaws stretched to engulf Me, and behind Me stalketh the lion of anger intent on tearing Me in pieces, and above Me, O My Well-Beloved, are the clouds of Thy decree, raining upon Me the showers of tribulations, whilst beneath Me are fixed the spears of misfortune, ready to wound My limbs and My body.*" "*Couldst thou be told,*" He further affirms, "*what hath befallen the Ancient Beauty, thou wouldst flee into the wilderness, and weep with a great weeping. In thy grief, thou wouldst smite thyself on the head, and cry out as one stung by the sting of the adder. . . . By the righteousness of God! Every morning I arose from My bed I discovered the hosts of countless afflictions massed behind My door, and every night when I lay down, lo! My heart was torn with agony at what it had suffered from the fiendish cruelty of its foes. With every piece of bread the Ancient Beauty breaketh is coupled the assault of a fresh affliction, and with every drop He drinketh is mixed the bitterness of the most woeful of trials. He is preceded in every step He taketh by an army of unforeseen calamities, while in His rear follow legions of agonizing sorrows.*"

Was it not He Who, at the early age of twenty-seven, spontaneously arose to champion, in the capacity of a mere follower, the nascent Cause of the Báb? Was He not the One Who by assuming the actual leadership of a proscribed and harassed sect exposed Himself, and His kindred, and His possessions, and His rank, and His reputation to the grave perils, the bloody assaults, the general spoliation and furious defamations of both government and people? Was it not He—the Bearer of a Revelation, Whose day *"every Prophet hath announced,"* for which *"the soul of every Divine Messenger hath thirsted,"* and in which *"God hath proved the hearts of the entire company of His Messengers and Prophets"*—was not the Bearer of such a Revelation, at the instigation of S͟hí‘ih ecclesiastics and by order of the S͟háh himself forced, for no less than four months, to breathe, in utter darkness, whilst in the company of the vilest criminals and freighted down with galling chains, the pestilential air of the vermin-infested subterranean dungeon of Ṭihrán—a place which, as He Himself subsequently declared, was mysteriously converted into the very scene of the annunciation made to Him by God of His Prophethood?

"We were consigned," He wrote in His "Epistle to 20
the Son of the Wolf," *"for four months to a place foul beyond comparison. As to the dungeon in which this Wronged One and others similarly wronged were confined, a dark and narrow pit were preferable. . . . The dungeon was wrapped in thick darkness, and Our fellow prisoners numbered nearly a hundred and fifty souls: thieves, assassins, and highwaymen. Though crowded, it had no other outlet than the passage by which We entered. No pen*

can depict that place, nor any tongue describe its loath-some smell. Most of these men had neither clothes nor bedding to lie on. God alone knoweth what befell Us in that most foul-smelling and gloomy place!" "'Abdu'l-Bahá," writes Dr. J. E. Esslemont, "tells how one day He was allowed to enter the prison-yard to see His beloved Father when He came out for His daily exercise. Bahá'u'lláh was terribly altered, so ill He could hardly walk. His hair and beard unkempt, His neck galled and swollen from the pressure of a heavy steel collar, His body bent by the weight of His chains." "For three days and three nights," Nabíl has recorded in his chronicle, "no manner of food or drink was given to Bahá'u'lláh. Rest and sleep were both impossible to Him. The place was infested with vermin, and the stench of that gloomy abode was enough to crush the very spirits of those who were condemned to suffer its horrors." "Such was the intensity of His suffering that the marks of that cruelty remained imprinted upon His body all the days of His life."

21   And what of the other tribulations which, before and immediately after this dreadful episode, touched Him? What of His confinement in the home of one of the kad-khudás of Ṭihrán? What of the savage violence with which He was stoned by the angry people in the neighborhood of the village of Níyálá? What of His incarceration by the emissaries of the army of the Sháh in Mázindarán, and His receiving the bastinado by order, and in the presence, of the assembled siyyids

and mujtahids into whose hands He had been delivered by the civil authorities of Ámul? What of the howls of derision and abuse with which a crowd of ruffians subsequently pursued Him? What of the monstrous accusation brought against Him by the Imperial household, the Court and the people, when the attempt was made on the life of Náṣiri'd-Dín Sháh? What of the infamous outrages, the abuse and ridicule heaped on Him when He was arrested by responsible officers of the government, and conducted from Níyávarán *on foot and in chains, with bared head and bare feet,* and exposed to the fierce rays of the midsummer sun, to the Síyáh-Chál of Ṭihrán? What of the avidity with which corrupt officials sacked His house and carried away all His possessions and disposed of His fortune? What of the cruel edict that tore Him from the small band of the Báb's bewildered, hounded, and shepherdless followers, separated Him from His kinsmen and friends, and banished Him, in the depth of winter, despoiled and defamed, to 'Iráq?

Severe as were these tribulations which succeeded 22 one another with bewildering rapidity as a result of the premeditated attacks and the systematic machinations of the court, the clergy, the government and the people, they were but the prelude to a harrowing and extensive captivity which that edict had formally initiated. Extending over a period of more than forty years, and carrying Him successively to 'Iráq, Sulaymáníyyih, Constantinople, Adrianople and finally to the penal colony of 'Akká, this long banishment was at last ended by His death, at the age of over three score years and ten, terminating a captivity which, in its range, its duration and the diversity and severity of its afflictions, is unexampled in the history of previous Dispensations.

23   No need to expatiate on the particular episodes which cast a lurid light on the moving annals of those years. No need to dwell on the character and actions of the peoples, rulers and divines who have participated in, and contributed to heighten the poignancy of the scenes of this, the greatest drama in the world's spiritual history.

Features of This Moving Drama

24   To enumerate a few of the outstanding features of this moving drama will suffice to evoke in the reader of these pages, already familiar with the history of the Faith, the memory of those vicissitudes which it has experienced, and which the world has until now viewed with such frigid indifference. The forced and sudden retirement of Bahá'u'lláh to the mountains of Sulaymáníyyih, and the distressing consequences that flowed from His two years' complete withdrawal; the incessant intrigues indulged in by the exponents of Shí'ih Islám in Najaf and Karbilá, working in close and constant association with their confederates in Persia; the

intensification of the repressive measures decreed by
Sulṭán ʿAbduʾl-ʿAzíz which brought to a head the defection of certain prominent members of the exiled
community; the enforcement of yet another banishment by order of that same Sulṭán, this time to that far
off and most desolate of cities, causing such despair as
to lead two of the exiles to attempt suicide; the
unrelaxing surveillance to which they were subjected
upon their arrival in ʿAkká, by hostile officials, and the
insufferable imprisonment for two years in the barracks of that town; the interrogatory to which the Turkish páshá subsequently subjected his Prisoner at the
headquarters of the government; His confinement for
no less than eight years in a humble dwelling sur-
rounded by the befouled air of that city, His sole rec-
reation being confined to pacing the narrow space of
His room—these, as well as other tribulations, proclaim, on the one hand, the nature of the ordeal and
the indignities He suffered, and point, on the other,
the finger of accusation at those mighty ones of the
earth who had either so sorely maltreated Him, or deliberately withheld from Him their succor.

No wonder that from the Pen of Him Who bore 25
this anguish with such sublime patience these words
should have been revealed: *"He Who is the Lord of the
seen and unseen is now manifest unto all men. His blessed
Self hath been afflicted with such harm that if all the seas,
visible and invisible, were turned into ink, and all that
dwell in the kingdom into pens, and all that are in the*

heavens and all that are on earth into scribes, they would, of a certainty, be powerless to record it." And again: *"I have been, most of the days of My life, even as a slave, sitting under a sword hanging on a thread, knowing not whether it would fall soon or late upon him." "All this generation,"* He affirms, *"could offer Us were wounds from its darts, and the only cup it proffered to Our lips was the cup of its venom. On Our neck We still bear the scar of chains, and upon Our body are imprinted the evidences of an unyielding cruelty." "Twenty years have passed, O kings! "* He, addressing the kings of Christendom, at the height of His mission, has written, *"during which We have, each day, tasted the agony of a fresh tribulation. No one of them that were before Us hath endured the things We have endured. Would that ye could perceive it! They that rose up against Us have put Us to death, have shed Our blood, have plundered Our property, and violated Our honor. Though aware of most of Our afflictions, ye, nevertheless, have failed to stay the hand of the aggressor. For is it not your clear duty to restrain the tyranny of the oppressor, and to deal equitably with your subjects, that your high sense of justice may be fully demonstrated to all mankind?"*

Who is the ruler, may it not be confidently asked, whether of the East or of the West, who, at any time since the dawn of so transcendent a Revelation, has been prompted to raise his voice either in its praise or against those who persecuted it? Which people has, in the course of so long a captivity, felt urged to arise and stem the tide of such tribulations? Who is the sovereign, excepting a single woman, shining in solitary glory, who has, in however small a measure, felt impelled to respond to the poignant call of Bahá'u'lláh? Who amongst the great ones of the earth was inclined to extend this infant Faith of God the benefit of his recognition or support? Which one of the multitudes of creeds, sects, races, parties and classes and of the highly diversified schools of human thought, considered it necessary to direct its gaze towards the rising light of the Faith, to contemplate its unfolding system, to ponder its hidden processes, to appraise its weighty message, to acknowledge its regenerative power, to embrace its salutary truth, or to proclaim its eternal verities? Who among the worldly wise and the so-called men of insight and wisdom can justly claim, after the lapse of nearly a century, to have disinterestedly approached its theme, to have considered impartially its claims, to have taken sufficient pains to delve into its literature, to have assiduously striven to separate facts from fiction, or to have accorded its cause the treatment it merits? Where are the preeminent exponents, whether of the arts or sciences, with the exception of a few isolated cases, who have lifted a finger, or whispered a word of commendation, in either the defense or the praise of a Faith that has conferred upon the world so priceless a benefit, that has suffered so long and so grievously, and which enshrines within its shell so enthralling a promise for a world so woefully battered, so manifestly bankrupt?

To the mounting tide of trials which laid low the 27

Báb, to the long-drawn-out calamities which rained on Bahá'u'lláh, to the warnings sounded by both the Herald and the Author of the Bahá'í Revelation, must be added the sufferings which, for no less than seventy years, were endured by 'Abdu'l-Bahá, as well as His pleas, and entreaties, uttered in the evening of His life, in connection with the dangers that increasingly threatened the whole of mankind. Born in the very year that witnessed the inception of the Bábí Revelation; baptized with the initial fires of persecution that raged around that nascent Cause; an eyewitness, when a boy of eight, of the violent upheavals that rocked the Faith which His Father had espoused; sharing with Him, the ignominy, the perils, and rigors consequent upon the successive banishments from His native land to countries far beyond its confines; arrested and forced to support, in a dark cell, the indignity of imprisonment soon after His arrival in 'Akká; the object of repeated investigations and the target of continual assaults and insults under the despotic rule of Sulṭán 'Abdu'l-Ḥamíd, and later under the ruthless military dictatorship of the suspicious and merciless Jamál Páshá—He, too, the Center and Pivot of Bahá'u'lláh's peerless Covenant and the perfect Exemplar of His teachings, was made to taste, at the hands of potentates, ecclesiastics, governments and peoples, the cup of woe which the Báb and Bahá'u'lláh, as well as so many of their followers, had drained.

28   With the warnings which both His pen and voice have given in countless Tablets and discourses, during

an almost lifelong incarceration and in the course of His extended travels in both the European and American continents, they who labor for the spread of His Father's Faith in the Western world are sufficiently acquainted. How often and how passionately did He appeal to those in authority and to the public at large to examine dispassionately the precepts enunciated by His Father? With what precision and emphasis He unfolded the system of the Faith He was expounding, elucidated its fundamental verities, stressed its distinguishing features, and proclaimed the redemptive character of its principles? How insistently did He foreshadow the impending chaos, the approaching upheavals, the universal conflagration which, in the concluding years of His life, had only begun to reveal the measure of its force and the significance of its impact on human society?

A co-sharer in the woeful trials and momentary frustrations afflicting the Báb and Bahá'u'lláh; reaping a harvest in His lifetime wholly incommensurate to the sublime, the incessant and strenuous efforts He had exerted; experiencing the initial perturbations of the world-shaking catastrophe in store for an unbelieving humanity; bent with age, and with eyes dimmed by the gathering storm which the reception accorded by a faithless generation to His Father's Cause was raising, and with a heart bleeding over the immediate destiny of God's wayward children—He, at last, sank beneath a weight of troubles for which they who had imposed them upon Him, and upon those gone before Him, were soon to be summoned to a dire reckoning.

30   *"Hasten, O my God!"* He cried, at a time when adversity had sore beset Him, *"the days of my ascension unto Thee, and of my coming before Thee, and of my entry into Thy presence, that I may be delivered from the darkness of the cruelty inflicted by them upon me, and may enter the luminous atmosphere of Thy nearness, O my Lord, the All-Glorious, and may rest under the shadow of Thy most great mercy."* *"Yá Bahá'u'l-Abhá* [O Thou the Glory of Glories]*!"* He wrote in a Tablet revealed during the last week of His life, *"I have renounced the world and the people thereof, and am heartbroken and sorely afflicted because of the unfaithful. In the cage of this world I flutter even as a frightened bird, and yearn every day to take my flight unto Thy Kingdom. Yá Bahá'u'l-Abhá! Make me to drink of the cup of sacrifice, and set me free. Relieve me from these woes and trials, from these afflictions and troubles."*

31   Dear friends! Alas, a thousand times alas, that a Revelation so incomparably great, so infinitely precious, so mightily potent, so manifestly innocent, should have received, at the hands of a generation so blind and so perverse, so infamous a treatment! *"O My servants!"* Bahá'u'lláh Himself testifies, *"The one true God is My witness! This most great, this fathomless and surging ocean is near, astonishingly near, unto you. Behold it is closer to you than your life vein! Swift as the twinkling of an eye ye can, if ye but wish it, reach and partake of this imperish-*

able favor, this God-given grace, this incorruptible gift,
this most potent and unspeakably glorious bounty."

A World Receded from Him

After a revolution of well nigh one hundred years what   32
is it that the eye encounters as one surveys the international scene and looks back upon the early beginnings
of Bahá'í history? A world convulsed by the agonies of
contending systems, races and nations, entangled in
the mesh of its accumulated falsities, receding farther
and farther from Him Who is the sole Author of its
destinies, and sinking deeper and deeper into a sui-
cidal carnage which its neglect and persecution of Him
Who is its Redeemer have precipitated. A Faith, still
proscribed, yet bursting through its chrysalis, emerg-
ing from the obscurity of a century-old repression, face
to face with the awful evidences of God's wrathful
anger, and destined to arise above the ruins of a smitten civilization. A world spiritually destitute, morally
bankrupt, politically disrupted, socially convulsed,
economically paralyzed, writhing, bleeding and break-
ing up beneath the avenging rod of God. A Faith Whose
call remained unanswered, Whose claims were rejected,
Whose warnings were brushed aside, Whose followers
were mowed down, Whose aims and purposes were
maligned, Whose summons to the rulers of the earth
were ignored, Whose Herald drained the cup of mar-

tyrdom, over the head of Whose Author swept a sea of unheard-of tribulations, and Whose Exemplar sank beneath the weight of lifelong sorrows and dire misfortunes. A world that has lost its bearings, in which the bright flame of religion is fast dying out, in which the forces of a blatant nationalism and racialism have usurped the rights and prerogatives of God Himself, in which a flagrant secularism—the direct offspring of irreligion—has raised its triumphant head and is protruding its ugly features, in which the *"majesty of kingship"* has been disgraced, and they who wore its emblems have, for the most part, been hurled from their thrones, in which the once all-powerful ecclesiastical hierarchies of Islám, and to a lesser extent those of Christianity, have been discredited, and in which the virus of prejudice and corruption is eating into the vitals of an already gravely disordered society. A Faith Whose institutions—the pattern and crowning glory of the age which is to come—have been ignored and in some instances trampled upon and uprooted, Whose unfolding system has been derided and partly suppressed and crippled, Whose rising Order—the sole refuge of a civilization in the embrace of doom—has been spurned and challenged, Whose Mother-Temple has been seized and misappropriated, and Whose *"House"*—the *"cynosure of an adoring world"*—has, through a gross miscarriage of justice, as witnessed by the world's highest tribunal, been delivered into the hands of, and violated by, its implacable enemies.

We are indeed living in an age which, if we would 33
correctly appraise it, should be regarded as one which
is witnessing a dual phenomenon. The first signalizes
the death pangs of an order, effete and godless, that
has stubbornly refused, despite the signs and portents
of a century-old Revelation, to attune its processes to
the precepts and ideals which that Heaven-sent Faith
proffered it. The second proclaims the birth pangs of
an Order, divine and redemptive, that will inevitably
supplant the former, and within Whose administrative structure an embryonic civilization, incomparable
and world-embracing, is imperceptibly maturing. The
one is being rolled up, and is crashing in oppression,
bloodshed, and ruin. The other opens up vistas of a
justice, a unity, a peace, a culture, such as no age has
ever seen. The former has spent its force, demonstrated
its falsity and barrenness, lost irretrievably its oppor-
tunity, and is hurrying to its doom. The latter, virile
and unconquerable, is plucking asunder its chains, and
is vindicating its title to be the one refuge within which
a sore-tried humanity, purged from its dross, can attain its destiny.

"Soon," Bahá'u'lláh Himself has prophesied, "will 34
the present-day order be rolled up, and a new one spread
out in its stead." And again: "By Myself! The day is approaching when We will have rolled up the world and all
that is therein, and spread out a new Order in its stead."
"The day is approaching when God will have raised up a
people who will call to remembrance Our days, who will

tell the tale of Our trials, who will demand the restitution of Our rights, from them who, without a tittle of evidence, have treated Us with manifest injustice."

35   Dear friends! For the trials which have afflicted the Faith of Bahá'u'lláh a responsibility appalling and inescapable rests upon those into whose hands the reins of civil and ecclesiastical authority were delivered. The kings of the earth and the world's religious leaders alike must primarily bear the brunt of such an awful responsibility. *"Everyone well knoweth,"* Bahá'u'lláh Himself testifies, *"that all the kings have turned aside from Him, and all the religions have opposed Him." "From time immemorial,"* He declares, *"they who have been outwardly invested with authority have debarred men from setting their faces towards God. They have disliked that men should gather together around the Most Great Ocean, inasmuch as they have regarded, and still regard, such a gathering as the cause of, and the motive for, the disruption of their sovereignty." "The kings,"* He moreover has written, *"have recognized that it was not in their interest to acknowledge Me, as have likewise the ministers and the divines, notwithstanding that My purpose hath been most explicitly revealed in the Divine Books and Tablets, and the True One hath loudly proclaimed that this Most Great Revelation hath appeared for the betterment of the world and the exaltation of the nations." "Gracious God!"* writes the Báb in the Dalá'il-i-Sab'ih (Seven Proofs) with reference to the *"seven powerful sovereigns ruling the world"* in His day, *"None of them hath been informed of His* [the Báb's] *Manifestation, and if informed, none*

hath believed in Him. Who knoweth, they may leave this world below full of desire, and without having realized that the thing for which they were waiting had come to pass. This is what happened to the monarchs that held fast unto the Gospel. They awaited the coming of the Prophet of God [Muḥammad], *and when He did appear, they failed to recognize Him. Behold how great are the sums which these sovereigns expend without even the slightest thought of appointing an official charged with the task of acquainting them in their own realms with the Manifestation of God! They would thereby have fulfilled the purpose for which they have been created. All their desires have been and are still fixed upon leaving behind them traces of their names.*" The Báb, moreover, in that same treatise, censuring the failure of the Christian divines to acknowledge the truth of Muḥammad's mission, makes this illuminating statement: "*The blame falleth upon their doctors, for if these had believed, they would have been followed by the mass of their countrymen. Behold then, that which hath come to pass! The learned men of Christendom are held to be learned by virtue of their safeguarding the teaching of Christ, and yet consider how they themselves have been the cause of men's failure to accept the Faith and attain unto salvation!*"

Recipients of the Message

It should not be forgotten that it was the kings of the earth and the world's religious leaders who, above all 36 other categories of men, were made the direct recipients of the Message proclaimed by both the Báb and Bahá'u'lláh. It was they who were deliberately addressed in numerous and historic Tablets, who were summoned to respond to the Call of God, and to whom were directed, in clear and forcible language, the appeals, the admonitions and warnings of His persecuted Messengers. It was they who, when the Faith was born, and later when its mission was proclaimed, were still, for the most part, wielding unquestioned and absolute civil and ecclesiastical authority over their subjects and followers. It was they who, whether glorying in the pomp and pageantry of a kingship as yet scarcely restricted by constitutional limitations, or entrenched within the strongholds of a seemingly inviolable ecclesiastical power, assumed ultimate responsibility for any wrongs inflicted by those whose immediate destinies they controlled. It would be no exaggeration to say that in most of the countries of the European and Asiatic continents absolutism, on the one hand, and complete subservience to ecclesiastical hierarchies, on the other, were still the outstanding features of the political and religious life of the masses. These, dominated and shackled, were robbed of the necessary freedom that would enable them to either appraise the claims and merits of the Message proffered to them, or to embrace unreservedly its truth.

37   Small wonder, then, that the Author of the Bahá'í Faith, and to a lesser degree its Herald, should have

directed at the world's supreme rulers and religious leaders the full force of Their Messages, and made them the recipients of some of Their most sublime Tablets, and invited them, in a language at once clear and insistent, to heed Their call. Small wonder that They should have taken the pains to unroll before their eyes the truths of Their respective Revelations, and should have expatiated on Their woes and sufferings. Small wonder that They should have stressed the preciousness of the opportunities which it was in the power of these rulers and leaders to seize, and should have warned them in ominous tones of the grave responsibilities which the rejection of God's Message would entail, and should have predicted, when rebuffed and refused, the dire consequences which such a rejection involved. Small wonder that He Who is the King of kings and Vicegerent of God Himself should, when abandoned, contemned and persecuted, have uttered this epigrammatic and momentous prophecy: *"From two ranks amongst men power hath been seized: kings and ecclesiastics."*

As to the kings and emperors who not only symbolized in their persons the majesty of earthly dominion but who, for the most part, actually held unchallengeable sway over the multitudes of their subjects, their relation to the Faith of Bahá'u'lláh constitutes one of the most illuminating episodes in the history of the Heroic and Formative Ages of that Faith. The Divine summons which embraced within its scope so large a number of the crowned heads of both Europe and Asia; the theme and language of the Messages that brought them into direct contact with the Source of God's Revelation; the nature of their reaction to so stupendous an impact; and the consequences which ensued and can still be witnessed today are the salient features of a subject upon which I can but inadequately touch, and which will be fully and befittingly treated by future Bahá'í historians.

The Emperor of the French, the most powerful ruler of his day on the European continent, Napoleon III; Pope Pius IX, the supreme head of the highest church in Christendom, and wielder of the scepter of both temporal and spiritual authority; the omnipotent Czar of the vast Russian Empire, Alexander II; the renowned Queen Victoria, whose sovereignty extended over the greatest political combination the world has witnessed; William I, the conqueror of Napoleon III, King of Prussia and the newly acclaimed monarch of a unified Germany; Francis Joseph, the autocratic king-emperor of the Austro-Hungarian monarchy, the heir of the far-famed Holy Roman Empire; the tyrannical 'Abdu'l-'Azíz, the embodiment of the concentrated power vested in the Sultanate and the Caliphate; the notorious Náṣiri'd-Dín Sháh, the despotic ruler of Persia and the mightiest potentate of Shí'ih Islám—in a word, most of the preeminent embodiments of power and of sovereignty in His day became, one by one, the object of Bahá'u'lláh's special attention, and were made to sustain, in varying degrees, the weight of the force communicated by His appeals and warnings.

It should be borne in mind, however, that Bahá'u'lláh has not restricted the delivery of His Message to a few individual sovereigns, however potent the scepters they severally wielded, and however vast the dominions which they ruled. All the kings of the earth have been collectively addressed by His Pen, appealed to, and warned, at a time when the star of His Revelation was mounting its zenith, and whilst He lay a prisoner in the hands, and in the vicinity of the court, of His royal enemy. In a memorable Tablet, designated as the Súriy-i-Mulúk (Súrih of Kings) in which the Sulṭán himself and his ministers, and the kings of Christendom, and the French and Persian Ambassadors accredited to the Sublime Porte, and the Muslim ecclesiastical leaders in Constantinople, and its wise men and its inhabitants, and the people of Persia, and the philosophers of the world have been specifically addressed and admonished, He thus directs His words to the entire company of the monarchs of East and West:

Tablets to the Kings

"O kings of the earth! Give ear unto the Voice of God, calling from this sublime, this fruit-laden Tree, that hath sprung out of the Crimson Hill, upon the holy Plain, in-

toning the words: 'There is none other God but He, the Mighty, the All-Powerful, the All-Wise.' . . . Fear God, O concourse of kings, and suffer not yourselves to be deprived of this most sublime grace. Fling away, then, the things ye possess, and take fast hold on the Handle of God, the Exalted, the Great. Set your hearts towards the Face of God, and abandon that which your desires have bidden you to follow, and be not of those who perish. Relate unto them, O servant, the story of 'Alí [the Báb], when He came unto them with truth, bearing His glorious and weighty Book, and holding in His hands a testimony and proof from God, and holy and blessed tokens from Him. Ye, however, O kings, have failed to heed the Remembrance of God in His days and to be guided by the lights which arose and shone forth above the horizon of a resplendent Heaven. Ye examined not His Cause when so to do would have been better for you than all that the sun shineth upon, could ye but perceive it. Ye remained careless until the divines of Persia—those cruel ones—pronounced judgment against Him, and unjustly slew Him. His spirit ascended unto God, and the eyes of the inmates of Paradise and the angels that are nigh unto Him wept sore by reason of this cruelty. Beware that ye be not careless henceforth as ye have been careless aforetime. Return, then, unto God, your Maker, and be not of the heedless. . . . My face hath come forth from the veils, and shed its radiance upon all that is in heaven and on earth; and yet, ye turned not towards Him, notwithstanding that ye were created for Him, O concourse of kings! Follow, therefore,

*that which I speak unto you, and hearken unto it with
your hearts, and be not of such as have turned aside. For
your glory consisteth not in your sovereignty, but rather in
your nearness unto God and your observance of His command as sent down in His holy and preserved Tablets.
Should any one of you rule over the whole earth, and over
all that lieth within it and upon it, its seas, its lands, its
mountains, and its plains, and yet be not remembered by
God, all these would profit him not, could ye but know
it. . . . Arise, then, and make steadfast your feet, and
make ye amends for that which hath escaped you, and set
then yourselves towards His holy Court, on the shore of
His mighty Ocean, so that the pearls of knowledge and
wisdom, which God hath stored up within the shell of His
radiant heart, may be revealed unto you. . . . Beware
lest ye hinder the breeze of God from blowing over your
hearts, the breeze through which the hearts of such as have
turned unto Him can be quickened. . . ."*

"Lay not aside the fear of God, O kings of the earth," [42]
He, in that same Tablet has revealed, "and beware that
ye transgress not the bounds which the Almighty hath fixed.
Observe the injunctions laid upon you in His Book, and
take good heed not to overstep their limits. Be vigilant,
that ye may not do injustice to anyone, be it to the extent
of a grain of mustard seed. Tread ye the path of justice, for
this, verily, is the straight path. Compose your differences,
and reduce your armaments, that the burden of your expenditures may be lightened, and that your minds and
hearts may be tranquilized. Heal the dissensions that di-

vide you, and ye will no longer be in need of any armaments except what the protection of your cities and territories demandeth. Fear ye God, and take heed not to outstrip the bounds of moderation, and be numbered among the extravagant. We have learned that you are increasing your outlay every year, and are laying the burden thereof on your subjects. This, verily, is more than they can bear, and is a grievous injustice. Decide justly between men, and be ye the emblems of justice amongst them. This, if ye judge fairly, is the thing that behooveth you, and beseemeth your station.

43   "Beware not to deal unjustly with anyone that appealeth to you, and entereth beneath your shadow. Walk ye in the fear of God, and be ye of them that lead a godly life. Rest not on your power, your armies, and treasures. Put your whole trust and confidence in God, Who hath created you, and seek ye His help in all your affairs. Succor cometh from Him alone. He succoreth whom He willeth with the hosts of the heavens and of the earth.

44   "Know ye that the poor are the trust of God in your midst. Watch that ye betray not His trust, that ye deal not unjustly with them and that ye walk not in the ways of the treacherous. Ye will most certainly be called upon to answer for His trust on the day when the Balance of Justice shall be set, the day when unto everyone shall be rendered his due, when the doings of all men, be they rich or poor, shall be weighed.

45   "If ye pay no heed unto the counsels which, in peerless and unequivocal language, We have revealed in this Tab-

let, Divine chastisement shall assail you from every direction, and the sentence of His justice shall be pronounced
against you. On that day ye shall have no power to resist
Him, and shall recognize your own impotence. Have mercy
on yourselves and on those beneath you, and judge ye between them according to the precepts prescribed by God in
His most holy and exalted Tablet, a Tablet wherein He
hath assigned to each and every thing its settled measure,
in which He hath given, with distinctness, an explanation of all things, and which is in itself a monition unto
them that believe in Him.

    "Examine Our Cause, inquire into the things that   46
have befallen Us, and decide justly between Us and Our
enemies, and be ye of them that act equitably towards
their neighbors. If ye stay not the hand of the oppressor, if
ye fail to safeguard the rights of the downtrodden, what
right have ye then to vaunt yourselves among men? What
is it of which ye can rightly boast? Is it on your food and
your drink that ye pride yourselves, on the riches ye lay up
in your treasuries, on the diversity and the cost of the ornaments with which ye deck yourselves? If true glory were
to consist in the possession of such perishable things, then
the earth on which ye walk must needs vaunt itself over
you, because it supplieth you, and bestoweth upon you,
these very things, by the decree of the Almighty. In its bowels
are contained, according to what God hath ordained, all
that ye possess. From it, as a sign of His mercy, ye derive
your riches. Behold then your state, the thing in which ye
glory! Would that ye could perceive it! Nay! By Him Who

*holdeth in His grasp the kingdom of the entire creation!
Nowhere doth your true and abiding glory reside except
in your firm adherence unto the precepts of God, your
wholehearted observance of His laws, your resolution to
see that they do not remain unenforced, and to pursue
steadfastly the right course. . . ."*

47   And again in that same Tablet: *"Twenty years have
passed, O kings, during which We have, each day, tasted
the agony of a fresh tribulation. No one of them that were
before Us hath endured the things We have endured.
Would that ye could perceive it! They that rose up against
Us, have put Us to death, have shed Our blood, have plundered Our property, and violated Our honor. Though
aware of most of Our afflictions, ye, nevertheless, have
failed to stay the hand of the aggressor. For is it not your
clear duty to restrain the tyranny of the oppressor, and to
deal equitably with your subjects, that your high sense of
justice may be fully demonstrated to all mankind?*

48   *"God hath committed into your hands the reins of
the government of the people, that ye may rule with justice over them, safeguard the rights of the downtrodden,
and punish the wrongdoers. If ye neglect the duty prescribed unto you by God in His Book, your names shall be
numbered with those of the unjust in His sight. Grievous,
indeed, will be your error. Cleave ye to that which your
imaginations have devised, and cast behind your backs
the commandments of God, the Most Exalted, the Inac-
cessible, the All-Compelling, the Almighty? Cast away the
things ye possess, and cling to that which God hath bid-*

den you observe. Seek ye His grace, for he that seeketh it treadeth His straight Path.

"*Consider the state in which We are, and behold ye* 49
the ills and troubles that have tried Us. Neglect Us not,
though it be for a moment, and judge ye between Us and
Our enemies with equity. This will, surely, be a mani-
fest advantage unto you. Thus do We relate to you Our
tale, and recount the things that have befallen Us, that
ye might take off Our ills and ease Our burden. Let him
who will, relieve Us from Our trouble; and as to him
that willeth not, my Lord is assuredly the best of Helpers.

"*Warn and acquaint the people, O Servant, with the* 50
things We have sent down unto Thee, and let the fear of
no one dismay Thee, and be Thou not of them that waver.
The day is approaching when God will have exalted His
Cause and magnified His testimony in the eyes of all who
are in the heavens and all who are on the earth. Place, in
all circumstances, Thy whole trust in Thy Lord, and fix
Thy gaze upon Him, and turn away from all them that
repudiate His truth. Let God, Thy Lord, be Thy sufficing
Succorer and Helper. We have pledged Ourself to secure
Thy triumph upon earth and to exalt Our Cause above
all men, though no king be found who would turn his
face towards Thee. . . ."

In the Kitáb-i-Aqdas (The Most Holy Book), that 51
priceless treasury enshrining for all time the brightest
emanations of the mind of Bahá'u'lláh, the Charter of
His World Order, the chief repository of His laws, the
Harbinger of His Covenant, the Pivotal Work con-

taining some of His noblest exhortations, weightiest pronouncements, and portentous prophecies, and revealed during the full tide of His tribulations, at a time when the rulers of the earth had definitely forsaken Him—in such a Book we read the following:

52   *"O kings of the earth! He Who is the sovereign Lord of all is come. The Kingdom is God's, the omnipotent Protector, the Self-Subsisting. Worship none but God, and, with radiant hearts, lift up your faces unto your Lord, the Lord of all names. This is a Revelation to which whatever ye possess can never be compared, could ye but know it. We see you rejoicing in that which ye have amassed for others, and shutting out yourselves from the worlds which naught except My Guarded Tablet can reckon. The treasures ye have laid up have drawn you far away from your ultimate objective. This ill beseemeth you, could ye but understand it. Wash your hearts from all earthly defilements, and hasten to enter the Kingdom of your Lord, the Creator of earth and heaven, Who caused the world to tremble, and all its peoples to wail, except them that have renounced all things and clung to that which the Hidden Tablet hath ordained. . . ."*

The Most Great Law Revealed

53 And further: *"O kings of the earth! The Most Great Law hath been revealed in this Spot, this Scene of transcendent splendor. Every hidden thing hath been brought to*

light, by virtue of the Will of the Supreme Ordainer, He Who hath ushered in the Last Hour, through Whom the Moon hath been cleft, and every irrevocable decree expounded.

"Ye are but vassals, O kings of the earth! He Who is   54
the King of Kings hath appeared, arrayed in His most wondrous glory, and is summoning you unto Himself, the Help in Peril, the Self-Subsisting. Take heed lest pride deter you from recognizing the Source of Revelation; lest the things of this world shut you out as by a veil from Him Who is the Creator of heaven. Arise, and serve Him Who is the Desire of all nations, Who hath created you through a word from Him, and ordained you to be, for all time, the emblems of His sovereignty.

"By the righteousness of God! It is not Our wish to   55
lay hands on your kingdoms. Our mission is to seize and possess the hearts of men. Upon them the eyes of Bahá are fastened. To this testifieth the Kingdom of Names, could ye but comprehend it. Whoso followeth his Lord, will renounce the world and all that is therein; how much greater, then, must be the detachment of Him Who holdeth so august a station! Forsake your palaces, and haste ye to gain admittance into His Kingdom. This, indeed, will profit you both in this world and in the next. To this testifieth the Lord of the realm on high, did ye but know it.

"How great is the blesssedness that awaiteth the king   56
who will arise to aid My Cause in My Kingdom, who will detach himself from all else but Me! Such a king is num-

bered with the companions of the Crimson Ark, the Ark which God hath prepared for the people of Bahá. All must glorify his name, must reverence his station, and aid him to unlock the cities with the keys of My Name, the omnipotent Protector of all that inhabit the visible and invisible kingdoms. Such a king is the very eye of mankind, the luminous ornament on the brow of creation, the fountainhead of blessings unto the whole world. Offer up, O people of Bahá, your substance, nay your very lives, for his assistance."

57   And further, this evident arraignment in that same Book: "*We have asked nothing from you. For the sake of God We, verily, exhort you, and will be patient as We have been patient in that which hath befallen Us at your hands, O concourse of kings!*"

58   Moreover, in His Tablet to Queen Victoria Bahá'u'lláh thus addresses all the kings of the earth, summoning them to cleave to the Lesser Peace, as distinct from that Most Great Peace which those who are fully conscious of the power of His Revelation and avowedly profess the tenets of His Faith can alone proclaim and must eventually establish:

59   "*O kings of the earth! We see you increasing every year your expenditures, and laying the burden thereof on your subjects. This, verily, is wholly and grossly unjust. Fear the sighs and tears of this Wronged One, and lay not excessive burdens on your peoples. Do not rob them to rear palaces for yourselves; nay rather choose for them that which ye choose for yourselves. Thus We unfold to your eyes that*

which profiteth you, if ye but perceive. Your people are your treasures. Beware lest your rule violate the commandments of God, and ye deliver your wards to the hands of the robber. By them ye rule, by their means ye subsist, by their aid ye conquer. Yet, how disdainfully ye look upon them! How strange, how very strange!

"Now that ye have refused the Most Great Peace, hold 60
ye fast unto this, the Lesser Peace, that haply ye may in some degree better your own condition and that of your dependents.

"O rulers of the earth! Be reconciled among your- 61
selves, that ye may need no more armaments save in a measure to safeguard your territories and dominions. Beware lest ye disregard the counsel of the All-Knowing, the Faithful.

"Be united, O kings of the earth, for thereby will the 62
tempest of discord be stilled amongst you, and your peoples find rest, if ye be of them that comprehend. Should anyone among you take up arms against another, rise ye all against him, for this is naught but manifest justice."

To the Christian kings Bahá'u'lláh, moreover, par- 63
ticularly directs His words of censure, and, in a language that cannot be mistaken, He discloses the true character of His Revelation:

"O kings of Christendom! Heard ye not the saying of 64
Jesus, the Spirit of God, 'I go away, and come again unto you'? Wherefore, then, did ye fail, when He did come again unto you in the clouds of heaven, to draw nigh unto Him, that ye might behold His face, and be of them that at-

tained His Presence? In another passage He saith: 'When He, the Spirit of Truth, is come, He will guide you into all truth.' And yet, behold how, when He did bring the truth, ye refused to turn your faces towards Him, and persisted in disporting yourselves with your pastimes and fancies. Ye welcomed Him not, neither did ye seek His presence, that ye might hear the verses of God from His own mouth, and partake of the manifold wisdom of the Almighty, the All-Glorious, the All-Wise. Ye have, by reason of your failure, hindered the breath of God from being wafted over you, and have withheld from your souls the sweetness of its fragrance. Ye continue roving with delight in the valley of your corrupt desires. Ye and all ye possess shall pass away. Ye shall, most certainly, return to God, and shall be called to account for your doings in the presence of Him Who shall gather together the entire creation. . . .*"

65   The Báb, moreover, in the Qayyúm-i-Asmá', His celebrated commentary on the Súrih of Joseph, revealed in the first year of His Mission, and characterized by Bahá'u'lláh as *"the first, the greatest, and mightiest of all books"* in the Bábí Dispensation, has issued this stirring call to the kings and princes of the earth:

66   *"O concourse of kings and of the sons of kings! Lay aside, one and all, your dominion which belongeth unto God. . . . Vain indeed is your dominion, for God hath set aside earthly possessions for such as have denied Him. . . . O concourse of kings! Deliver with truth and in all haste the verses sent down by Us to the peoples of Turkey and of India, and beyond them, with power and with truth, to lands in both the East and the West. . . . By God! If ye do*

well, to your own behoof will ye do well; and if ye deny God and His signs, We, in very truth, having God, can well dispense with all creatures and all earthly dominion."

And again: *"Fear ye God, O concourse of kings, lest ye remain afar from Him Who is His Remembrance [the Báb], after the Truth hath come unto you with a Book and signs from God, as spoken through the wondrous tongue of Him Who is His Remembrance. Seek ye grace from God, for God hath ordained for you, after ye have believed in Him, a Garden the vastness of which is as the vastness of the whole of Paradise."* 67

So much for the epoch-making counsels and warnings collectively addressed by the Báb and Bahá'u'lláh to the sovereigns of the earth, and more particularly directed to the kings of Christendom. I would be failing to do justice to my theme were I to ignore, or even to dismiss briefly, those audacious, fate-laden apostrophes to individual monarchs who, whether as kings or emperors, have either viewed with cold indifference the tribulations, or rejected with contempt the warnings, of the twin Founders of our Faith. I can neither quote as fully as I should from the two thousand and more verses that have streamed from the pen of Bahá'u'lláh and, to a lesser extent, from that of the Báb, addressed to individual monarchs in Europe and Asia, nor is it my purpose to expatiate upon the circumstances that have provoked, or the consequences that have flowed from, those astounding utterances. The historian of the future, viewing more widely and 68 in fuller perspective the momentous happenings of the Apostolic and Formative Ages of the Faith of Bahá'u'lláh, will no doubt be able to evaluate accurately and to describe in a circumstantial manner the causes, the implications and the effects of these Divine Messages which, in their scope and effectiveness, have certainly no parallel in the religious annals of mankind.

69   To the French Emperor, Napoleon III, Bahá'u'lláh addressed these words: *"O King of Paris! Tell the priest to ring the bells no longer. By God, the True One! The Most Mighty Bell hath appeared in the form of Him Who is the Most Great Name, and the fingers of the will of thy Lord, the Most Exalted, the Most High, toll it out in the heaven of Immortality, in His Name, the All-Glorious. Thus have the mighty verses of thy Lord been again sent down unto thee, that thou mayest arise to remember God, the Creator of earth and heaven, in these days when all the tribes of the earth have mourned, and the foundations of the cities have trembled, and the dust of irreligion hath enwrapped all men, except such as thy Lord, the All-Knowing, the All-Wise, was pleased to spare. . . . Give ear, O King, unto the Voice that calleth from the Fire which burneth in this Verdant Tree, upon this Sinai which hath been raised above the hallowed and snow-white Spot, beyond the Everlasting City: 'Verily, there is none other God but Me, the Ever-Forgiving, the Most Merciful!' We, in truth, have sent Him Whom We aided with the Holy Spirit* [Jesus], *that He may announce unto you this Light that hath shown forth from the horizon of the will*

of your Lord, the Most Exalted, the All-Glorious, and Whose signs have been revealed in the West, that ye may set your faces towards Him [Bahá'u'lláh], on this Day which God hath exalted above all other days, and whereon the All-Merciful hath shed the splendor of His effulgent glory upon all who are in heaven and all who are on earth. Arise thou to serve God and help His Cause. He, verily, will assist thee with the hosts of the seen and unseen, and will set thee king over all that whereon the sun riseth. Thy Lord, in truth, is the All-Powerful, the Almighty. . . . Attire thy temple with the ornament of My Name, and thy tongue with remembrance of Me, and thine heart with love for Me, the Almighty, the Most High. We have desired for thee naught except that which is better for thee than what thou dost possess and all the treasures of the earth. Thy Lord, verily, is knowing, informed of all. . . .

"O King! We heard the words thou didst utter in answer to the Czar of Russia, concerning the decision made regarding the war [Crimean War]. Thy Lord, verily, knoweth, is informed of all. Thou didst say: 'I lay asleep upon my couch, when the cry of the oppressed, who were drowned in the Black Sea, wakened me.' This is what we heard thee say, and, verily, thy Lord is witness unto what I say. We testify that that which wakened thee was not their cry, but the promptings of thine own passions, for We tested thee, and found thee wanting. Comprehend the meaning of My words, and be thou of the discerning. . . . Hadst thou been sincere in thy words, thou wouldst have *not cast behind thy back the Book of God, when it was sent unto thee by Him Who is the Almighty, the All-Wise. We have proved thee through it, and found thee other than that which thou didst profess. Arise, and make amends for that which escaped thee. Erelong the world and all that thou possessest will perish, and the kingdom will remain unto God, thy Lord and the Lord of thy fathers of old. It behooveth thee not to conduct thine affairs according to the dictates of thy desires. Fear the sighs of this Wronged One, and shield Him from the darts of such as act unjustly. For what thou hast done, thy kingdom shall be thrown into confusion, and thine empire shall pass from thine hands, as a punishment for that which thou hast wrought. Then wilt thou know how thou hast plainly erred. Commotions shall seize all the people in that land, unless thou arisest to help this Cause, and followest Him Who is the Spirit of God [Jesus] in this, the straight Path. Hath thy pomp made thee proud? By My Life! It shall not endure; nay, it shall soon pass away, unless thou holdest fast by this firm Cord. We see abasement hastening after thee, while thou art of the heedless. . . . Abandon thy palaces to the people of the graves, and thine empire to whosoever desireth it, and turn, then, unto the Kingdom. This, verily, is what God hath chosen for thee, wert thou of them that turn unto Him. . . . Shouldst thou desire to bear the weight of thy dominion, bear it then to aid the Cause of thy Lord. Glorified be this station which whoever attaineth thereunto hath attained unto all good that proceedeth from Him Who is the All-*

*Knowing, the All-Wise. . . . Exultest thou over the trea-
sures thou dost possess, knowing they shall perish? Rejoic-
est thou in that thou rulest a span of earth, when the
whole world, in the estimation of the people of Bahá, is
worth as much as the black in the eye of a dead ant?
Abandon it unto such as have set their affections upon it,
and turn thou unto Him Who is the Desire of the world.
Whither are gone the proud and their palaces? Gaze thou
into their tombs, that thou mayest profit by this example,
inasmuch as We made it a lesson unto every beholder. Were
the breezes of Revelation to seize thee, thou wouldst flee
the world, and turn unto the Kingdom, and wouldst expend all thou possessest, that thou mayest draw nigh unto
this sublime Vision."*

Revealed to the Pope

To Pope Pius IX, Bahá'u'lláh revealed the following: 71
*"O Pope! Rend the veils asunder. He Who is the Lord of
Lords is come overshadowed with clouds, and the decree hath been fulfilled by God, the Almighty, the Unre-
strained. . . . He, verily, hath again come down from
Heaven even as He came down from it the first time. Beware that thou dispute not with Him even as the Pharisees disputed with Him* [Jesus] *without a clear token or
proof. On His right hand flow the living waters of grace,
and on His left the choice Wine of justice, whilst before
Him march the angels of Paradise, bearing the banners of*

His signs. Beware lest any name debar thee from God, the
Creator of earth and heaven. Leave thou the world behind thee, and turn towards thy Lord, through Whom the
whole earth hath been illumined. . . . Dwellest thou in
palaces whilst He Who is the King of Revelation liveth in
the most desolate of abodes? Leave them unto such as desire them, and set thy face with joy and delight towards
the Kingdom. . . . Arise in the name of thy Lord, the God
of Mercy, amidst the peoples of the earth, and seize thou
the Cup of Life with the hands of confidence, and first
drink thou therefrom, and proffer it then to such as turn
towards it amongst the peoples of all faiths. . . .

72   "Call thou to remembrance Him Who was the Spirit
[Jesus], Who, when He came, the most learned of His age
pronounced judgment against Him in His own country,
whilst he who was only a fisherman believed in Him.
Take heed, then, ye men of understanding heart! Thou,
in truth, art one of the suns of the heaven of His names.
Guard thyself, lest darkness spread its veils over thee, and
fold thee away from His light. . . . Consider those who
opposed the Son [Jesus], when He came unto them with
sovereignty and power. How many the Pharisees who
were waiting to behold Him, and were lamenting over
their separation from Him! And yet, when the fragrance
of His coming was wafted over them, and His beauty was
unveiled, they turned aside from Him and disputed with
Him. . . . None save a very few, who were destitute of any
power amongst men, turned towards His face. And yet
today every man endowed with power and invested with

sovereignty prideth himself on His Name! In like manner,
consider how numerous, in these days, are the monks who,
in My Name, have secluded themselves in their churches,
and who, when the appointed time was fulfilled, and
We unveiled Our beauty, knew Us not, though they call
upon Me at eventide and at dawn. . . .

"*The Word which the Son concealed is made mani-*   73
fest. It hath been sent down in the form of the human
temple in this day. Blessed be the Lord Who is the Father!
He, verily, is come unto the nations in His most great
majesty. Turn your faces towards Him, O concourse of the
righteous! . . . This is the day whereon the Rock [Peter]
crieth out and shouteth, and celebrateth the praise of its
Lord, the All-Possessing, the Most High, saying: 'Lo! The
Father is come, and that which ye were promised in the
Kingdom is fulfilled! . . .' My body longeth for the cross,
and Mine head waiteth the thrust of the spear, in the
path of the All-Merciful, that the world may be purged
from its transgressions. . . .

"*O Supreme Pontiff! Incline thine ear unto that which*   74
the Fashioner of moldering bones counseleth thee, as voiced
by Him Who is His Most Great Name. Sell all the embel-
lished ornaments thou dost possess, and expend them in
the path of God, Who causeth the night to return upon the
day, and the day to return upon the night. Abandon thy
kingdom unto the kings, and emerge from thy habita-
tion, with thy face set towards the Kingdom, and, de-
tached from the world, then speak forth the praises of thy
Lord betwixt earth and heaven. Thus hath bidden thee

He Who is the Possessor of Names, on the part of thy Lord, the Almighty, the All-Knowing. Exhort thou the kings and say: 'Deal equitably with men. Beware lest ye transgress the bounds fixed in the Book.' This indeed becometh thee. Beware lest thou appropriate unto thyself the things of the world and the riches thereof. Leave them unto such as desire them, and cleave unto that which hath been enjoined upon thee by Him Who is the Lord of creation. Should anyone offer thee all the treasures of the earth, refuse to even glance upon them. Be as thy Lord hath been. Thus hath the Tongue of Revelation spoken that which God hath made the ornament of the book of creation. . . . Should the inebriation of the wine of My verses seize thee, and thou determinest to present thyself before the throne of thy Lord, the Creator of earth and heaven, make My love thy vesture, and thy shield remembrance of Me, and thy provision reliance upon God, the Revealer of all power. . . . Verily, the day of ingathering is come, and all things have been separated from each other. He hath stored away that which He chose in the vessels of justice, and cast into fire that which befitteth it. Thus hath it been decreed by your Lord, the Mighty, the Loving, in this promised Day. He, verily, ordaineth what He pleaseth. There is none other God save He, the Almighty, the All-Compelling."

75   In the Tablet addressed to the Czar of Russia, Alexander II, we read: *"O Czar of Russia! Incline thine ear unto the voice of God, the King, the Holy, and turn thou unto Paradise, the Spot wherein abideth He Who, among the Concourse on high, beareth the most excellent*

titles, and Who, in the kingdom of creation, is called by the name of God, the Effulgent, the All-Glorious. Beware lest thy desire deter thee from turning towards the face of thy Lord, the Compassionate, the Most Merciful. We, verily, have heard the thing for which thou didst supplicate thy Lord, whilst secretly communing with Him. Wherefore, the breeze of My loving-kindness wafted forth, and the sea of My mercy surged, and We answered thee in truth. Thy Lord, verily, is the All-Knowing, the All-Wise. Whilst I lay chained and fettered in the prison, one of thy ministers extended Me his aid. Wherefore hath God ordained for thee a station which the knowledge of none can comprehend except His knowledge. Beware lest thou barter away this sublime station. . . . Beware lest thy sovereignty withhold thee from Him Who is the Supreme Sovereign. He, verily, is come with His Kingdom, and all the atoms cry aloud: 'Lo! The Lord is come in His great majesty!' He Who is the Father is come, and the Son [Jesus], in the holy vale, crieth out: 'Here am I, here am I, O Lord, My God!', whilst Sinai circleth round the House, and the Burning Bush calleth aloud: 'The All-Bounteous is come mounted upon the clouds! Blessed is he that draweth nigh unto Him, and woe betide them that are far away.'

"Arise thou amongst men in the name of this all-compelling Cause, and summon, then, the nations unto God, the Exalted, the Great. Be thou not of them who called upon God by one of His names, but who, when He Who is the Object of all names appeared, denied Him and turned aside from Him, and, in the end, pronounced sentence *against Him with manifest injustice. Consider and call thou to mind the days whereon the Spirit of God* [Jesus] *appeared, and Herod gave judgment against Him. God, however, aided Him with the hosts of the unseen, and protected Him with truth, and sent Him down unto another land, according to His promise. He, verily, ordaineth what He pleaseth. Thy Lord truly preserveth whom He willeth, be he in the midst of the seas, or in the maw of the serpent, or beneath the sword of the oppressor. . . .*

77   *"Again I say: Hearken unto My voice that calleth from My prison, that it may acquaint thee with the things that have befallen My Beauty, at the hands of them that are the manifestations of My glory, and that thou mayest perceive how great hath been My patience, notwithstanding My might, and how immense My forbearance, notwithstanding My power. By My life! Couldst thou but know the things sent down by My Pen, and discover the treasures of My Cause, and the pearls of My mysteries which lie hid in the seas of My names and in the goblets of My words, thou wouldst, in thy love for My name, and in thy longing for My glorious and sublime Kingdom, lay down thy life in My path. Know thou that though My body be beneath the swords of My foes, and My limbs be beset with incalculable afflictions, yet My spirit is filled with a gladness with which all the joys of the earth can never compare.*

78   *"Set thine heart towards Him Who is the Point of adoration for the world, and say: O peoples of the earth! Have ye denied the One in Whose path He Who came*

*with the truth, bearing the announcement of your Lord,
the Exalted, the Great, suffered martyrdom? Say: This is
an Announcement whereat the hearts of the Prophets and
Messengers have rejoiced. This is the One Whom the heart
of the world remembereth, and is promised in the Books of
God, the Mighty, the All-Wise. The hands of the Messengers were, in their desire to meet Me, upraised towards
God, the Mighty, the Glorified. . . . Some lamented in
their separation from Me, others endured hardships in
My path, and still others laid down their lives for the sake
of My Beauty, could ye but know it. Say: I, verily, have
not sought to extol Mine Own Self, but rather God Himself, were ye to judge fairly. Naught can be seen in Me
except God and His Cause, could ye but perceive it. I am
the One Whom the tongue of Isaiah hath extolled, the
One with Whose name both the Torah and the Evangel
were adorned. . . . Blessed be the king whose sovereignty
hath withheld him not from his Sovereign, and who hath
turned unto God with his heart. He, verily, is accounted
of those that have attained unto that which God, the
Mighty, the All-Wise, hath willed. Erelong will such a
one find himself numbered with the monarchs of the realms
of the Kingdom. Thy Lord is, in truth, potent over all
things. He giveth what He willeth to whomsoever He
willeth, and withholdeth what He pleaseth from whomsoever He willeth. He, verily, is the All-Powerful, the Almighty."*

To Queen Victoria Bahá'u'lláh has written: *"O
Queen in London! Incline thine ear unto the voice of thy* 79

Lord, the Lord of all mankind, calling from the Divine Lote-Tree: Verily, no God is there but Me, the Almighty, the All-Wise! Cast away all that is on earth, and attire the head of thy kingdom with the crown of the remembrance of thy Lord, the All-Glorious. He, in truth, hath come unto the world in His most great glory, and all that hath been mentioned in the Gospel hath been fulfilled. The land of Syria hath been honored by the footsteps of its Lord, the Lord of all men, and north and south are both inebriated with the wine of His presence. Blessed is the man that inhaled the fragrance of the Most Merciful, and turned unto the Dawning-Place of His Beauty, in this resplendent Dawn. The Mosque of Aqṣá vibrateth through the breezes of its Lord, the All-Glorious, whilst Baṭḥá [Mecca] trembleth at the voice of God, the Exalted, the Most High. Whereupon every single stone of them celebrateth the praise of the Lord, through this Great Name.

80   *"Lay aside thy desire, and set then thine heart towards thy Lord, the Ancient of Days. We make mention of thee for the sake of God, and desire that thy name may be exalted through thy remembrance of God, the Creator of earth and heaven. He, verily, is witness unto that which I say. We have been informed that thou hast forbidden the trading in slaves, both men and women. This, verily, is what God hath enjoined in this wondrous Revelation. God hath, truly, destined a reward for thee, because of this. He, verily, will pay the doer of good his due recompense, wert thou to follow what hath been sent unto thee by Him Who is the All-Knowing, the All-Informed. As to*

him who turneth aside, and swelleth with pride, after that the clear tokens have come unto him, from the Revealer of signs, his work shall God bring to naught. He, in truth, hath power over all things. Man's actions are acceptable after his having recognized [the Manifestation]. *He that turneth aside from the True One is indeed the most veiled amongst His creatures. Thus hath it been decreed by Him Who is the Almighty, the Most Powerful.*

  "We have also heard that thou hast entrusted the reins 81 *of counsel into the hands of the representatives of the people. Thou, indeed, hast done well, for thereby the foundations of the edifice of thine affairs will be strengthened, and the hearts of all that are beneath thy shadow, whether high or low, will be tranquilized. It behooveth them, however, to be trustworthy among His servants, and to regard themselves as the representatives of all that dwell on earth. This is what counseleth them, in this Tablet, He Who is the Ruler, the All-Wise. . . . Blessed is he that entereth the assembly for the sake of God, and judgeth between men with pure justice. He, indeed, is of the blissful. . . .*

  "Turn thou unto God and say: O my Sovereign Lord! 82 *I am but a vassal of Thine, and Thou art, in truth, the King of kings. I have lifted my suppliant hands unto the heaven of Thy grace and Thy bounties. Send down, then, upon me from the clouds of Thy generosity that which will rid me of all save Thee, and draw me nigh unto Thyself. I beseech Thee, O my Lord, by Thy name, which Thou hast made the king of names and the manifestation of Thyself to all who are in heaven and on earth, to rend*

asunder the veils that have intervened between me and my recognition of the Dawning-Place of Thy signs and the Dayspring of Thy Revelation. Thou art, verily, the Almighty, the All-Powerful, the All-Bounteous. Deprive me not, O my Lord, of the fragrances of the Robe of Thy mercy in Thy days, and write down for me that which Thou hast written down for Thy handmaidens who have believed in Thee and in Thy signs, and have recognized Thee, and set their hearts towards the horizon of Thy Cause. Thou art truly the Lord of the worlds and of those who show mercy the Most Merciful. Assist me, then, O my God, to remember Thee amongst Thy handmaidens, and to aid Thy Cause in Thy lands. Accept, then, that which hath escaped me when the light of Thy countenance shone forth. Thou, indeed, hast power over all things. Glory be to Thee, O Thou in Whose hand is the kingdom of the heavens and of the earth."

83   In the Kitáb-i-Aqdas, His Most Holy Book, Bahá'u'lláh thus addresses the German Emperor, William I: *"Say: O King of Berlin! Give ear unto the Voice calling from this manifest Temple: Verily, there is none other God but Me, the Everlasting, the Peerless, the Ancient of Days. Take heed lest pride debar thee from recognizing the Dayspring of Divine Revelation, lest earthly desires shut thee out, as by a veil, from the Lord of the Throne above and of the earth below. Thus counseleth thee the Pen of the Most High. He, verily, is the Most Gracious, the All-Bountiful. Do thou remember the one whose power transcended thy power* [Napoleon III], *and*

whose station excelled thy station. Where is he? Whither are gone the things he possessed? Take warning, and be not of them that are fast asleep. He it was who cast the Tablet of God behind him, when We made known unto him what the hosts of tyranny had caused Us to suffer. Wherefore, disgrace assailed him from all sides, and he went down to dust in great loss. Think deeply, O King, concerning him, and concerning them who, like unto thee, have conquered cities and ruled over men. The All-Merciful brought them down from their palaces to their graves. Be warned, be of them who reflect."

And further, in that same Book, this remarkable 84 prophecy: *"O banks of the Rhine! We have seen you covered with gore, inasmuch as the swords of retribution were drawn against you; and you shall have another turn. And We hear the lamentations of Berlin, though she be today in conspicuous glory."*

Again in the Kitáb-i-Aqdas these words, directed 85 to Emperor Francis Joseph, are recorded: *"O Emperor of Austria! He Who is the Dayspring of God's Light dwelt in the prison of 'Akká, at the time when thou didst set forth to visit the Aqṣá Mosque* [Jerusalem]. *Thou passed Him by, and inquired not about Him, by Whom every house is exalted, and every lofty gate unlocked. We, verily, made it* [Jerusalem] *a place whereunto the world should turn, that they might remember Me, and yet thou hast rejected Him Who is the Object of this remembrance, when He appeared with the Kingdom of God, thy Lord and the Lord of the worlds. We have been with thee at all* times, and found thee clinging unto the Branch and heedless of the Root. Thy Lord, verily, is a witness unto what I say. We grieved to see thee circle round Our Name, whilst unaware of Us, though We were before thy face. Open thine eyes, that thou mayest behold this glorious Vision, and recognize Him Whom thou invokest in the daytime and in the night season, and gaze on the Light that shineth above this luminous Horizon."

86 In the Súriy-i-Mulúk Sulṭán 'Abdu'l-'Azíz is addressed in the following terms: *"Hearken, O king, to the speech of Him that speaketh the truth, Him that doth not ask thee to recompense Him with the things God hath chosen to bestow upon thee, Him Who unerringly treadeth the straight Path. He it is Who summoneth thee unto God, thy Lord, Who showeth thee the right course, the way that leadeth to true felicity, that haply thou mayest be of them with whom it shall be well. . . . He that giveth up himself wholly to God, God shall, assuredly, be with him; and he that placeth his complete trust in God, God shall, verily, protect him from whatsoever may harm him, and shield him from the wickedness of every evil plotter.*

87 *"Wert thou to incline thine ear unto My speech and observe My counsel, God would exalt thee to so eminent a position that the designs of no man on the whole earth could ever touch or hurt thee. Observe, O king, with thine inmost heart and with thy whole being, the precepts of God, and walk not in the paths of the oppressor. Seize thou, and hold firmly within the grasp of thy might, the*

reins of the affairs of thy people, and examine in person whatever pertaineth unto them. Let nothing escape thee, for therein lieth the highest good.

"*Render thanks unto God for having chosen thee out of the whole world, and made thee king over them that profess thy faith. It well beseemeth thee to appreciate the wondrous favors with which God hath favored thee, and to magnify continually His name. Thou canst best praise Him if thou lovest His loved ones, and dost safeguard and protect His servants from the mischief of the treacherous, that none may any longer oppress them. Thou shouldst, moreover, arise to enforce the law of God amongst them, that thou mayest be of those who are firmly established in His law.* 88

"*Shouldst thou cause rivers of justice to spread their waters amongst thy subjects, God would surely aid thee with the hosts of the unseen and of the seen, and would strengthen thee in thine affairs. No God is there but Him. All creation and its empire are His. Unto Him return the works of the faithful.* 89

"*Place not thy reliance on thy treasures. Put thy whole confidence in the grace of God, thy Lord. Let Him be thy trust in whatever thou doest, and be of them that have submitted themselves to His Will. Let Him be thy helper and enrich thyself with His treasures, for with Him are the treasuries of the heavens and of the earth. He bestoweth them upon whom He will, and from whom He will He withholdeth them. There is none other God but Him, the All-Possessing, the All-Praised. All are but paupers at the* 90 door of His mercy; all are helpless before the revelation of His sovereignty, and beseech His favors.

91   "Overstep not the bounds of moderation, and deal justly with them that serve thee. Bestow upon them according to their needs, and not to the extent that will enable them to lay up riches for themselves, to deck their persons, to embellish their homes, to acquire the things that are of no benefit unto them, and to be numbered with the extravagant. Deal with them with undeviating justice, so that none among them may either suffer want, or be pampered with luxuries. This is but manifest justice. Allow not the abject to rule over and dominate them who are noble and worthy of honor, and suffer not the high-minded to be at the mercy of the contemptible and worthless, for this is what We observed upon Our arrival in the City [Constantinople], and to it We bear witness. . . .

92   "Set before thine eyes God's unerring Balance and, as one standing in His Presence, weigh in that balance thine actions every day, every moment of thy life. Bring thyself to account ere thou art summoned to a reckoning, on the Day when no man shall have strength to stand for fear of God, the Day when the hearts of the heedless ones shall be made to tremble. . . .

93   "Thou art God's shadow on earth. Strive, therefore, to act in such a manner as befitteth so eminent, so august a station. If thou dost depart from following the things We have caused to descend upon thee and taught thee, thou wilt, assuredly, be derogating from that great and price-

less honor. Return, then, and cleave wholly unto God, and cleanse thine heart from the world and all its vanities, and suffer not the love of any stranger to enter and dwell therein. Not until thou dost purify thine heart from every trace of such love can the brightness of the light of God shed its radiance upon it, for to none hath God given more than one heart. This, verily, hath been decreed and written down in His ancient Book. And as the human heart, as fashioned by God, is one and undivided, it behooveth thee to take heed that its affections be, also, one and undivided. Cleave thou, therefore, with the whole affection of thine heart, unto His love, and withdraw it from the love of anyone besides Him, that He may aid thee to immerse thyself in the ocean of His unity, and enable thee to become a true upholder of His oneness. . . .

Let the Oppressor Desist

"Let thine ear be attentive, O King, to the words We have 94 *addressed thee. Let the oppressor desist from his tyranny, and cut off the perpetrators of injustice from among them that profess thy faith. By the righteousness of God! The tribulations We have sustained are such that any pen that recounteth them cannot but be overwhelmed with anguish. No one of them that truly believe and uphold the unity of God can bear the burden of their recital. So great have been Our sufferings that even the eyes of our enemies have wept over Us, and beyond them those of every discerning*

person. And to all these trials have We been subjected, in spite of Our action in approaching thee, and in bidding the people to enter beneath thy shadow, that thou mightest be a stronghold unto them that believe in and uphold the unity of God.

95 *"Have I, O King, ever disobeyed thee? Have I, at any time, transgressed any of thy laws? Can any of thy ministers that represent thee in 'Iráq produce any proof that can establish My disloyalty to thee? No, by Him Who is the Lord of all worlds! Not for one short moment did We rebel against thee, or against any of thy ministers. Never, God willing, shall We revolt against thee, though We be exposed to trials more severe than any We suffered in the past. In the daytime and in the night season, at even and at morn, We pray to God on thy behalf, that He may graciously aid thee to be obedient unto Him and to observe His commandments, that He may shield thee from the hosts of the evil ones. Do, therefore, as it pleaseth thee, and treat Us as befitteth thy station and beseemeth thy sovereignty. Be not forgetful of the law of God in whatever thou desirest to achieve, now or in the days to come. Say: Praise be to God, the Lord of all worlds!"*

96 Moreover, in the Kitáb-i-Aqdas, is this vehement apostrophe to Constantinople: *"O Spot that art situate on the shores of the two seas! The throne of tyranny hath, verily, been stablished upon thee, and the flame of hatred hath been kindled within thy bosom, in such wise that the Concourse on high and they who circle around the Exalted Throne have wailed and lamented. We behold in*

thee the foolish ruling over the wise, and darkness vaunt-
ing itself against the light. Thou art indeed filled with
manifest pride. Hath thine outward splendor made thee
vainglorious? By Him Who is the Lord of mankind! It
shall soon perish, and thy daughters and thy widows and
all the kindreds that dwell within thee shall lament. Thus
informeth thee the All-Knowing, the All-Wise."

As to Náṣiri'd-Dín Sháh, the Lawḥ-i-Sulṭán, des-   97
patched to him from 'Akká and constituting Bahá'-
u'lláh's lengthiest Epistle to any single sovereign, proclaims: *"O King! I was but a man like others, asleep upon*
My couch, when lo, the breezes of the All-Glorious were
wafted over Me, and taught Me the knowledge of all that
hath been. This thing is not from Me, but from One Who
is Almighty and All-Knowing. And He bade Me lift up
My voice between earth and heaven, and for this there
befell Me what hath caused the tears of every man of un-
derstanding to flow. The learning current amongst men I
studied not; their schools I entered not. Ask of the city
wherein I dwelt, that thou mayest be well assured that I
am not of them who speak falsely. This is but a leaf which
the winds of the will of thy Lord, the Almighty, the All-
Praised, have stirred. Can it be still when the tempestu-
ous winds are blowing? Nay, by Him Who is the Lord of
all Names and Attributes! They move it as they list. The
evanescent is as nothing before Him Who is the Ever-Abid-
ing. His all-compelling summons hath reached Me, and
caused Me to speak His praise amidst all people. I was
indeed as one dead when His behest was uttered. The

hand of the will of thy Lord, the Compassionate, the Merciful, transformed Me. Can anyone speak forth of his own accord that for which all men, both high and low, will protest against him? Nay, by Him Who taught the Pen the eternal mysteries, save him whom the grace of the Almighty, the All-Powerful, hath strengthened. The Pen of the Most High addresseth Me saying: Fear not. Relate unto His Majesty the <u>Shah</u> that which befell thee. His heart, verily, is between the fingers of thy Lord, the God of Mercy, that haply the sun of justice and bounty may shine forth above the horizon of his heart. Thus hath the decree been irrevocably fixed by Him Who is the All-Wise.

98   "Look upon this Youth, O King, with the eyes of justice; judge thou, then, with truth concerning what hath befallen Him. Of a verity, God hath made thee His shadow amongst men, and the sign of His power unto all that dwell on earth. Judge thou between Us and them that have wronged Us without proof and without an enlightening Book. They that surround thee love thee for their own sakes, whereas this Youth loveth thee for thine own sake, and hath had no desire except to draw thee nigh unto the seat of grace, and to turn thee toward the right hand of justice. Thy Lord beareth witness unto that which I declare.

99   "O King! Wert thou to incline thine ear unto the shrill of the Pen of Glory and the cooing of the Dove of Eternity which, on the branches of the Lote-Tree beyond which there is no passing, uttereth praises to God, the Maker of all names and Creator of earth and heaven,

thou wouldst attain unto a station from which thou wouldst behold in the world of being naught save the effulgence of the Adored One, and wouldst regard thy sovereignty as the most contemptible of thy possessions, abandoning it to whosoever might desire it, and setting thy face toward the Horizon aglow with the light of His countenance. Neither wouldst thou ever be willing to bear the burden of dominion save for the purpose of helping thy Lord, the Exalted, the Most High. Then would the Concourse on high bless thee. O how excellent is this most sublime station, couldst thou ascend thereunto through the power of a sovereignty recognized as derived from the Name of God! . . .

"O King of the age! The eyes of these refugees are 100 *turned towards and fixed upon the mercy of the Most Merciful. No doubt is there whatever that these tribulations will be followed by the outpourings of a supreme mercy, and these dire adversities be succeeded by an overflowing prosperity. We fain would hope, however, that His Majesty the Sháh will himself examine these matters, and bring hope to the hearts. That which We have submitted to thy Majesty is indeed for thine highest good. And God, verily, is a sufficient witness unto Me. . . .*

"O would that thou wouldst permit Me, O Sháh, to 101 *send unto thee that which would cheer the eyes, and tranquilize the souls, and persuade every fair-minded person that with Him is the knowledge of the Book. . . . But for the repudiation of the foolish and the connivance of the divines, I would have uttered a discourse that would have*

thrilled and carried away the hearts unto a realm from the murmur of whose winds can be heard: 'No God is there but He!' . . .

102   "I have seen, O Sháh, in the path of God what eye hath not seen nor ear heard. . . . How numerous the tribulations which have rained, and will soon rain, upon Me! I advance with My face set towards Him Who is the Almighty, the All-Bounteous, whilst behind Me glideth the serpent. Mine eyes have rained down tears until My bed is drenched. I sorrow not for Myself, however. By God! Mine head yearneth for the spear out of love for its Lord. I never passed a tree, but Mine heart addressed it saying: 'O would that thou wert cut down in My name, and My body crucified upon thee, in the path of My Lord!' . . . By God! Though weariness lay Me low, and hunger consume Me, and the bare rock be My bed, and My fellows the beasts of the field, I will not complain, but will endure patiently as those endued with constancy and firmness have endured patiently, through the power of God, the Eternal King and Creator of the nations, and will render thanks unto God under all conditions. We pray that, out of His bounty—exalted be He—He may release, through this imprisonment, the necks of men from chains and fetters, and cause them to turn, with sincere faces, towards His Face, Who is the Mighty, the Bounteous. Ready is He to answer whosoever calleth upon Him, and nigh is He unto such as commune with Him."

103   In the Qayyúm-i-Asmá' the Báb, for His part, thus addresses Muhammad Sháh: "O King of Islám! Aid thou,

with the truth, after having aided the Book, Him Who is
Our Most Great Remembrance, for God hath, in very
truth, destined for thee, and for such as circle round thee,
on the Day of Judgment, a responsible position in His
Path. I swear by God, O Sháh! If thou showest enmity
unto Him Who is His Remembrance, God will, on the
Day of Resurrection, condemn thee, before the kings, unto
hellfire, and thou shalt not, in very truth, find on that
Day any helper except God, the Exalted. Purge thou, O
Sháh, the Sacred Land [Ṭihrán] *from such as have repu-*
diated the Book, ere the day whereon the Remembrance of
God cometh, terribly and of a sudden, with His potent
Cause, by the leave of God, the Most High. God, verily,
hath prescribed to thee to submit unto Him Who is His
Remembrance, and unto His Cause, and to subdue, with
the truth and by His leave, the countries, for in this world
thou hast been mercifully invested with sovereignty, and
will, in the next, dwell, nigh unto the Seat of Holiness,
with the inmates of the Paradise of His good pleasure. Let
not thy sovereignty deceive thee, O Sháh, for 'every soul
shall taste of death,' and this, in very truth, hath been
written down as a decree of God."

In His Tablet to Muḥammad Sháh the Báb, more- 104
over, has revealed: *"I am the Primal Point from which*
have been generated all created things. I am the Counte-
nance of God Whose splendor can never be obscured, the
Light of God Whose radiance can never fade. . . . All
the keys of heaven God hath chosen to place on My right
hand, and all the keys of hell on My left. . . . I am one of

the sustaining pillars of the Primal Word of God. Whosoever hath recognized Me, hath known all that is true
and right, and hath attained all that is good and
seemly. . . . The substance wherewith God hath created
Me is not the clay out of which others have been formed.
He hath conferred upon Me that which the worldly-wise
can never comprehend, nor the faithful discover. . . .

105   "By My life! But for the obligation to acknowledge
the Cause of Him Who is the Testimony of God . . . I
would not have announced this unto thee. . . . In that
same year [year 60] I despatched a messenger and a book
unto thee, that thou mightest act towards the Cause of
Him Who is the Testimony of God as befitteth the station
of thy sovereignty. . . .

106   "I swear by the truth of God! Were he who hath been
willing to treat Me in such a manner to know who it is
whom he hath so treated, he, verily, would never in his
life be happy. Nay—I, verily, acquaint thee with the truth
of the matter—it is as if he hath imprisoned all the Prophets, and all the men of truth, and all the chosen ones. . . .
Woe betide him from whose hands floweth evil, and blessed
the man from whose hands floweth good. . . .

107   "I swear by God! I seek no earthly goods from thee,
be it as much as a mustard seed. . . . I swear by the truth
of God! Wert thou to know that which I know, thou
wouldst forego the sovereignty of this world and of the
next, that thou mightest attain My good pleasure, through
thine obedience unto the True One. . . . Wert thou to
refuse, the Lord of the world would raise up one who will

exalt His Cause, and the Command of God will, verily,
be carried into effect."

God's Vicar on Earth

Dear friends! How vast a panorama these gemlike, these   108
soul-searching divinely uttered pronouncements out-
spread before our eyes! What memories they evoke!
How sublime the principles they inculcate! What hopes
they engender! What apprehensions they excite! And
yet how fragmentary must these above-quoted words,
suited as they are to the immediate purpose of my
theme, appear when compared with the torrential
majesty which only the reading of the full text can
disclose! He Who was God's Vicar on earth, addressing, at the most critical moment when His Revelation
was attaining it zenith, those who concentrated in their
persons the splendor, the sovereignty, and the strength
of earthly dominion, could certainly not subtract one
jot or tittle from the weight and force which the pre-
sentation of so historic a Message demanded. Neither
the perils which were fast closing in upon Him, nor
the formidable power with which the doctrine of absolute sovereignty invested, at that time, the emperors
of the West and the potentates of the East, could restrain the Exile and Prisoner of Adrianople from com-
municating the full blast of His Message to His twin
imperial persecutors as well as to the rest of their fellow-sovereigns.

109   The magnitude and diversity of the theme, the cogency of the argument, the sublimity and audacity of the language, arrest our attention and astound our minds. Emperors, kings and princes, chancellors and ministers, the Pope himself, priests, monks and philosophers, the exponents of learning, parliamentarians and deputies, the rich ones of the earth, the followers of all religions, and the people of Bahá—all are brought within the purview of the Author of these Messages, and receive, each according to their merits, the counsels and admonitions they deserve. No less amazing is the diversity of the subjects touched upon in these Tablets. The transcendent majesty and unity of an unknowable and unapproachable God is extolled, the oneness of His Messengers proclaimed and emphasized. The uniqueness, the universality and potentialities of the Bahá'í Faith are stressed, and the purpose and character of the Bábí Revelation unfolded. The significance of Bahá'u'lláh's sufferings and banishments is disclosed, and the tribulations rained down upon His Herald and upon His Namesake recognized and lamented. His own yearning for the crown of martyrdom, which they both so mysteriously won, is voiced, and the ineffable glories and wonders in store for His own Dispensation foreshadowed. Episodes, at once moving and marvelous, at various stages of His ministry, are recounted, and the transitoriness of worldly pomp, fame, riches, and sovereignty, repeatedly and categorically asserted. Appeals for the application of the highest principles in human and international relations are forcibly and

insistently made, and the abandonment of discreditable practices and conventions, detrimental to the happiness, the growth, the prosperity and the unity of the human race, enjoined. Kings are censured, ecclesiastical dignitaries arraigned, ministers and plenipotentiaries condemned, and the identification of His advent with the coming of the Father Himself unequivocally admitted and repeatedly announced. The violent downfall of a few of these kings and emperors is prophesied, two of them are definitely challenged, most are warned, all are appealed to and exhorted.

In the Lawḥ-i-Sulṭán (Tablet to the Sháh of Persia) Bahá'u'lláh declares: *"Would that the world-adorning wish of His Majesty might decree that this Servant be brought face to face with the divines of the age, and produce proofs and testimonies in the presence of His Majesty the Sháh! This Servant is ready, and taketh hope in God, that such a gathering may be convened in order that the truth of the matter may be made clear and manifest before His Majesty the Sháh. It is then for thee to command, and I stand ready before the throne of thy sovereignty. Decide, then, for Me or against Me."* 110

And moreover, in the Lawḥ-i-Ra'ís, Bahá'u'lláh, recalling His conversation with the Turkish officer charged with the task of enforcing His banishment to the fortress-town of 'Akká, has written: *"There is a matter, which, if thou findest it possible, I request thee to submit to His Majesty the Sulṭán, that for ten minutes this Youth be enabled to meet him, so that he may demand whatsoever he deemeth as a sufficient testimony and* 111

*regardeth as proof of the veracity of Him Who is the Truth.
Should God enable Him to produce it, let him, then, release these wronged ones, and leave them to themselves."*
"*He promised,*" Bahá'u'lláh adds in that Tablet, "*to trans-
mit this message, and to give Us his reply. We received,
however, no news from him. Although it becometh not
Him Who is the Truth to present Himself before any person, inasmuch as all have been created to obey Him, yet
in view of the condition of these little children and the
large number of women so far removed from their friends
and countries, We have acquiesced in this matter. In spite
of this nothing hath resulted. 'Umar himself is alive and
accessible. Inquire from him, that the truth may be made
known unto you.*"

112   Referring to these Tablets addressed to the sovereigns of the earth, and which 'Abdu'l-Bahá has acclaimed as a "*miracle,*" Bahá'u'lláh has written: "*Each
one of them hath been designated by a special name. The
first hath been named 'The Rumbling,' the second, 'The
Blow,' the third, 'The Inevitable,' the fourth, 'The Plain,'
the fifth, 'The Catastrophe,' and the others, 'The Stun-
ning Trumpet Blast,' 'The Near Event,' 'The Great Terror,'
'The Trumpet,' 'The Bugle,' and their like, so that all the
peoples of the earth may know, of a certainty, and may
witness, with outward and inner eyes, that He Who is the
Lord of Names hath prevailed, and will continue to prevail, under all conditions, over all men. . . . Never since
the beginning of the world hath the Message been so openly
proclaimed. . . . Glorified be this Power which hath shone*

forth and compassed the worlds! This act of the Causer of Causes hath, when revealed, produced two results. It hath at once sharpened the swords of the infidels, and unloosed the tongues of such as have turned towards Him in His remembrance and praise. This is the effect of the fertilizing winds, mention of which hath been made aforetime in the Lawḥ-i-Haykal. The whole earth is now in a state of pregnancy. The day is approaching when it will have yielded its noblest fruits, when from it will have sprung forth the loftiest trees, the most enchanting blossoms, the most heavenly blessings. Immeasurably exalted is the breeze that wafteth from the garment of thy Lord, the Glorified! For lo, it hath breathed its fragrance and made all things new! Well is it with them that comprehend. It is indubitably clear and evident that in these things He Who is the Lord of Revelation hath sought nothing for Himself. Though aware that they would lead to tribulations, and be the cause of troubles and afflictive trials, He, solely as a token of His loving-kindness and favor, and for the purpose of quickening the dead and of manifesting the Cause of the Lord of all Names and Attributes, and of redeeming all who are on earth, hath closed His eyes to His own well-being and borne that which no other person hath borne or will bear."

The most important of His Tablets addressed to individual sovereigns Bahá'u'lláh ordered to be written in the form of a pentacle, symbolizing the temple of man, including therein, as a conclusion, the following words which reveal the importance He attached to 113 those Messages, and indicate their direct association with the prophecy of the Old Testament: *"Thus have We built the Temple with the hands of power and might, could ye but know it. This is the Temple promised unto you in the Book. Draw ye nigh unto it. This is that which profiteth you, could ye but comprehend it. Be fair, O peoples of the earth! Which is preferable, this, or a temple which is built of clay? Set your faces towards it. Thus have ye been commanded by God, the Help in Peril, the Self-Subsisting. Follow ye His bidding, and praise ye God, your Lord, for that which He hath bestowed upon you. He, verily, is the Truth. No God is there but He. He revealeth what He pleaseth, through His words 'Be and it is.'"*

114   Referring to this same subject, He, in one of His Tablets, thus addresses the followers of Jesus Christ: *"O concourse of the followers of the Son! Verily, the Temple hath been built with the hands of the will of your Lord, the Almighty, the All-Bounteous. Bear, then, witness, O people, unto that which I say: Which is preferable, that which is built of clay, or that which is built by the hands of your Lord, the Revealer of verses? This is the Temple promised unto you in the Tablets. It calleth aloud: 'O followers of religions! Haste ye to attain unto Him Who is the Source of all causes, and follow not every infidel and doubter.'"*

115   It should not be forgotten that, apart from these specific Tablets in which the kings of the earth are severally and collectively addressed, Bahá'u'lláh has revealed other Tablets—the Lawḥ-i-Raʼís being an out-

standing example—and interspersed the mass of His voluminous writings with unnumbered passages, in which direct addresses, as well as references, have been made to ministers, governments, and their accredited representatives. I am not concerned, however, with such addresses and references, which, vital as they are, cannot be regarded as being endowed with that peculiar pregnancy which direct and specific messages, voiced by the Manifestation of God and directed to the world's Chief Magistrates in His day, must possess.

Dear friends! Enough has been said to portray the 116 tribulations which, for so long a time, overwhelmed the Founders of so preeminent a Revelation, and which the world has so disastrously ignored. Sufficient attention has also been directed to the Messages addressed to those sovereign rulers who, either in the exercise of their unconditioned authority, have deliberately provoked these sufferings, or could have, in the plenitude of their power, arisen to mitigate their effect or deflect their tragic course. Let us now consider the consequences that have ensued. The reaction of these monarchs was, as already stated, varied and unmistakable and, as the march of events has gradually unfolded, disastrous in its consequences. One of the most outstanding amongst these sovereigns treated the Divine Summons with gross disrespect, dismissing it with a curt and insolent reply, written by one of his ministers. Another laid violent hold on the bearer of the Message, tortured, branded, and brutally slew him.

Others preferred to maintain a contemptuous silence. All failed completely in their duty to arise and extend their assistance. Two of them, in particular, prompted by the dual impulse of fear and anger, tightened their grip on the Cause they had jointly resolved to uproot. The one condemned his Divine Prisoner to yet another banishment, to *"the most unsightly of cities in appearance, the most detestable in climate, and the foulest in water,"* whilst the other, powerless to lay hands on the Prime Mover of a hated Faith, subjected its adherents under his sway to abject and savage cruelties. The recital of Bahá'u'lláh's sufferings, embodied in those Messages, failed to evoke compassion in their hearts. His appeals, the like of which neither the annals of Christianity nor even those of Islám have recorded, were disdainfully rejected. The dark warnings He uttered were haughtily scorned. The bold challenges He issued were ignored. The chastisements He predicted they derisively brushed aside.

117   What, then—might we not consider—has, in the face of so complete and ignominious a rejection, happened, and is still happening, in the course, and particularly in the closing years, of this, the first Bahá'í century, a century fraught with such tumultuous sufferings and violent outrages for the persecuted Faith of Bahá'u'lláh? Empires fallen in dust, kingdoms subverted, dynasties extinguished, royalty besmirched, kings assassinated, poisoned, driven into exile, subjugated in their own realms, whilst the few remaining

thrones are trembling with the repercussions of the fall of their fellows.

This process, so gigantic, so catastrophic, may be 118 said to have had its inception on that memorable night when, in an obscure corner of Shíráz, the Báb, in the presence of the first Letter to believe in Him, revealed the first chapter of His celebrated commentary on the Súrih of Joseph (The Qayyúm-i-Asmá'), in which He trumpeted His Call to the sovereigns and princes of the earth. It passed from incubation to visible manifestation when Bahá'u'lláh's prophecies, enshrined for all time in the Súriy-i-Haykal, and uttered before Napoleon III's dramatic downfall and the self-imposed imprisonment of Pope Pius IX in the Vatican, were fulfilled. It gathered momentum when, in the days of 'Abdu'l-Bahá, the Great War extinguished the Romanov, the Hohenzollern, and Hapsburg dynasties, and converted powerful time-honored monarchies into republics. It was further accelerated, soon after 'Abdu'l-Bahá's passing, by the demise of the effete Qájár dynasty in Persia, and the stupendous collapse of both the Sultanate and the Caliphate. It is still operating, under our very eyes, as we behold the fate which, in the course of this colossal and ravaging struggle, is successively overtaking the crowned heads of the European continent. Surely, no man, contemplating dispassionately the manifestations of this relentless revolutionizing process, within comparatively so short a time, can escape the conclusion that the last hundred years may well be regarded, in so far as the fortunes of royalty are concerned, as one of the most cataclysmic periods in the annals of mankind.

Humiliation
Immediate and Complete

119 Of all the monarchs of the earth, at the time when Bahá'u'lláh, proclaiming His Message to them, revealed the Súriy-i-Mulúk in Adrianople, the most august and influential were the French Emperor and the Supreme Pontiff. In the political and religious spheres they respectively held the foremost rank, and the humiliation both suffered was alike immediate and complete.

120   Napoleon III, son of Louis Bonaparte (brother of Napoleon I), was, few historians will deny, the most outstanding monarch of his day in the West. "The Emperor," it was said of him, "was the state." The French capital was the most attractive capital in Europe, the French court "the most brilliant and luxurious of the XIXth century." Possessed of a fixed and indestructible ambition, he aspired to emulate the example, and finish the interrupted work, of his imperial uncle. A dreamer, a conspirator, of a shifting nature, hypocritical and reckless, he, the heir to the Napoleonic throne, taking advantage of the policy which sought to foster the reviving interest in the career of his great prototype, had sought to overthrow the monarchy. Failing in his attempt, he was deported to America, was later

captured in the course of an attempted invasion of
France, was condemned to perpetual captivity, and
escaped to London, until, in 1848, the Revolution
brought about his return, and enabled him to overthrow the constitution, after which he was proclaimed
emperor. Though able to initiate far-reaching movements, he possessed neither the sagacity nor the courage required to control them.

To this man, the last emperor of the French, who,   121
through foreign conquest, had striven to endear his
dynasty to the people, who even cherished the ideal of
making France the center of a revived Roman Empire—to such a man the Exile of 'Akká, already thrice
banished by Sultán 'Abdu'l-'Azíz, had transmitted, from
behind the walls of the barracks in which He lay imprisoned, an Epistle which bore this indubitably clear
arraignment and ominous prophecy: *"We testify that
that which wakened thee was not their cry* [Turks
drowned in the Black Sea], *but the promptings of thine
own passions, for We tested thee, and found thee wanting.
. . . Hadst thou been sincere in thy words, thou wouldst
not have cast behind thy back the Book of God* [previous
Tablet], *when it was sent unto thee by Him Who is the
Almighty, the All-Wise. . . . For what thou hast done,
thy kingdom shall be thrown into confusion, and thine
empire shall pass from thine hands, as a punishment for
that which thou hast wrought."*

Bahá'u'lláh's previous Message, forwarded through   122
one of the French ministers to the Emperor, had been

accorded a welcome the nature of which can be con-
jectured from the words recorded in the "Epistle to the
Son of the Wolf": *"To this* [first Tablet], *however, he
did not reply. After Our arrival in the Most Great Prison
there reached Us a letter from his minister, the first part
of which was in Persian, and the latter in his own hand-
writing. In it he was cordial, and wrote the following: 'I
have, as requested by you, delivered your letter, and until
now have received no answer. We have, however, issued
the necessary recommendations to our Minister in Constantinople and our consuls in those regions. If there be
anything you wish done, inform us, and we will carry it
out.' From his words it became apparent that he understood the purpose of this Servant to have been a request
for material assistance."*

123   In His first Tablet Bahá'u'lláh, wishing to test the
sincerity of the Emperor's motives, and deliberately
assuming a meek and unprovocative tone, had, after
expatiating on the sufferings He had endured, addressed him the following words: *"Two statements graciously uttered by the king of the age have reached the ears
of these wronged ones. These pronouncements are, in truth,
the king of all pronouncements, the like of which have
never been heard from any sovereign. The first was the
answer given the Russian government when it inquired
why the war* [Crimean] *was waged against it. Thou didst
reply: 'The cry of the oppressed who, without guilt or blame,
were drowned in the Black Sea wakened me at dawn.
Wherefore, I took up arms against thee.' These oppressed*

ones, however, have suffered a greater wrong, and are in greater distress. Whereas the trials inflicted upon those people lasted but one day, the troubles borne by these servants have continued for twenty and five years, every moment of which has held for us a grievous affliction. The other weighty statement, which was indeed a wondrous statement, manifested to the world, was this: 'Ours is the responsibility to avenge the oppressed and succor the helpless.' The fame of the Emperor's justice and fairness hath brought hope to a great many souls. It beseemeth the king of the age to inquire into the condition of such as have been wronged, and it behooveth him to extend his care to the weak. Verily, there hath not been, nor is there now, on earth anyone as oppressed as we are, or as helpless as these wanderers."

It is reported that upon receipt of this first Message that superficial, tricky, and pride-intoxicated monarch flung down the Tablet saying: "If this man is God, I am two gods!" The transmitter of the second Tablet had, it is reliably stated, in order to evade the strict surveillance of the guards, concealed it in his hat, and was able to deliver it to the French agent, who resided in 'Akká, and who, as attested by Nabíl in his Narrative, translated it into French and sent it to the Emperor, he himself becoming a believer when he had later witnessed the fulfillment of so remarkable a prophecy. 124

The significance of the somber and pregnant words uttered by Bahá'u'lláh in His second Tablet was soon 125 revealed. He who was actuated in provoking the Crimean War by his selfish desires, who was prompted by a personal grudge against the Russian Emperor, who was impatient to tear up the Treaty of 1815 in order to avenge the disaster of Moscow, and who sought to shed military glory over his throne, was soon himself engulfed by a catastrophe that hurled him in the dust, and caused France to sink from her preeminent station among the nations to that of a fourth power in Europe.

126   The Battle of Sedan in 1870 sealed the fate of the French Emperor. The whole of his army was broken up and surrendered, constituting the greatest capitulation hitherto recorded in modern history. A crushing indemnity was exacted. He himself was taken prisoner. His only son, the Prince Imperial, was killed, a few years later, in the Zulu War. The Empire collapsed, its program unrealized. The Republic was proclaimed. Paris was subsequently besieged and capitulated. "The terrible Year" marked by civil war, exceeding in its ferocity the Franco-German War, followed. William I, the Prussian king, was proclaimed German Emperor in the very palace which stood as a "mighty monument and symbol of the power and pride of Louis XIV, a power which had been secured to some extent by the humiliation of Germany." Deposed by a disaster "so appalling that it resounded throughout the world," this false and boastful monarch suffered in the end, and till his death, the same exile as that which, in the case of Bahá'u'lláh, he had so heartlessly ignored.

A humiliation less spectacular yet historically more 127 significant awaited Pope Pius IX. It was to him who regarded himself as the Vicar of Christ that Bahá'u'lláh wrote that *"the Word which the Son* [Jesus] *concealed is made manifest,"* that *"it hath been sent down in the form of the human temple,"* that the Word was Himself, and He Himself the Father. It was to him who styling himself "the servant of the servants of God" that the Promised One of all ages, unveiling His station in its plenitude, announced that *"He Who is the Lord of Lords is come overshadowed with clouds."* It was he, who, claiming to be the successor of St. Peter, was reminded by Bahá'u'lláh that *"this is the day whereon the Rock* [Peter] *crieth out and shouteth . . . saying: 'Lo, the Father is come, and that which ye were promised in the Kingdom is fulfilled.'"* It was he, the wearer of the triple crown, who later became the first prisoner of the Vatican, who was commanded by the Divine Prisoner of 'Akká to *"leave his palaces unto such as desire them,"* to *"sell all the embellished ornaments"* he possessed, and to *"expend them in the path of God,"* and to *"abandon his kingdom unto the kings,"* and emerge from his habitation with his face *"set towards the Kingdom."*

Count Mastai-Ferretti, Bishop of Imola, the 254th 128 pope since the inception of St. Peter's primacy, who had been elevated to the apostolic throne two years after the Declaration of the Báb, and the duration of whose pontificate exceeded that of any of his predecessors, will be permanently remembered as the author of the Bull which declared the Immaculate Conception of the Blessed Virgin (1854), referred to in the Kitáb-i-Íqán, to be a doctrine of the Church, and as the promulgator of the new dogma of Papal Infallibility (1870). Authoritarian by nature, a poor statesman, disinclined to conciliation, determined to preserve all his authority, he, while he succeeded through his assumption of an ultramontane attitude in defining further his position and in reinforcing his spiritual authority, failed, in the end, to maintain that temporal rule which, for so many centuries, had been exercised by the heads of the Catholic Church.

129   This temporal power had, throughout the ages, shrunk to insignificant proportions. The decades preceding its extinction were fraught with the gravest vicissitudes. As the sun of Bahá'u'lláh's Revelation was mounting to full meridian splendor, the shadows that beset the dwindling patrimony of St. Peter were correspondingly deepening. The Tablet of Bahá'u'lláh, addressed to Pius IX, precipitated its extinction. A hasty glance at the course of its ebbing fortunes, during those decades, will suffice. Napoleon I had driven the Pope from his estates. The Congress of Vienna had reestablished him as their head and their administration in the hands of the priests. Corruption, disorganization, impotence to ensure internal security, the restoration of the inquisition, had induced an historian to assert that "no land of Italy, perhaps of Europe, except Turkey, is ruled as is this ecclesiastical state." Rome was "a

city of ruins, both material and moral." Insurrections led to Austria's intervention. Five great Powers demanded the introduction of far-reaching reforms, which the Pope promised but failed to carry out. Austria again reasserted herself, and was opposed by France. Both watched each other on the Papal estates until 1838, when, on their withdrawal, absolutism was again restored. The Pope's temporal power was now denounced by some of his own subjects, heralding its extinction in 1870. Internal complications forced him to flee, in the dead of night and in the disguise of a humble priest, from Rome which was declared a republic. It was later restored by the French to its former status. The creation of the kingdom of Italy, the shifting policy of Napoleon III, the disaster of Sedan, the misdeeds of the Papal government denounced by Clarendon, at the Congress of Paris, terminating the Crimean War, as a "disgrace to Europe," sealed the fate of that tottering dominion.

In 1870, after Bahá'u'lláh had revealed His Epistle 130 to Pius IX, King Victor Emmanuel II went to war with the Papal states, and his troops entered Rome and seized it. On the eve of its seizure, the Pope repaired to the Lateran and, despite his age and with his face bathed in tears, ascended on bended knees the Scala Santa. The following morning, as the cannonade began, he ordered the white flag to be hoisted above the dome of St. Peter. Despoiled, he refused to recognize this "creation of revolution," excommunicated the invaders of his states, denounced Victor Emmanuel as the "robber King" and as "forgetful of every religious principle, despising every right, trampling upon every law." Rome, "the Eternal City, on which rest twenty-five centuries of glory," and over which the Popes had ruled in unchallengeable right for ten centuries, finally became the seat of the new kingdom, and the scene of that humiliation which Bahá'u'lláh had anticipated and which the Prisoner of the Vatican had imposed upon himself.

131   "The last years of the old Pope," writes a commentator on his life, "were filled with anguish. To his physical infirmities was added the sorrow of beholding, all too often, the Faith outraged in the very heart of Rome, the religious orders despoiled and persecuted, the Bishops and priests debarred from exercising their functions."

132   Every effort to retrieve the situation created in 1870 proved fruitless. The Archbishop of Posen went to Versailles to solicit Bismarck's intervention in behalf of the Papacy, but was coldly received. Later a Catholic party was organized in Germany to bring political pressure on the German Chancellor. All, however, was in vain. The mighty process already referred to had to pursue inexorably its course. Even now, after the lapse of above half a century, the so-called restoration of temporal sovereignty has but served to throw into greater relief the helplessness of this erstwhile potent Prince, at whose name kings trembled and to whose

dual sovereignty they willingly submitted. This temporal sovereignty, practically confined to the minuscule City of the Vatican, and leaving Rome the undisputed possession of a secular monarchy, has been obtained at the price of unreserved recognition, so long withheld, of the Kingdom of Italy. The Treaty of the Lateran, claiming to have resolved once and for all the Roman Question, has indeed assured to a secular Power, in respect of the Enclaved City, a liberty of action which is fraught with uncertainty and peril. "The two souls of the Eternal City," a Catholic writer has observed, "have been separated from each other, only to collide more severely than ever before."

Well might the Sovereign Pontiff recall the reign 133 of the most powerful among his predecessors, Innocent III who, during the eighteen years of his pontificate, raised and deposed the kings and the emperors, whose interdicts deprived nations of the exercise of Christian worship, at the feet of whose legate the King of England surrendered his crown, and at whose voice the fourth and the fifth crusades were both undertaken.

Might not the process, to which reference has already been made, manifest, in the course of its operation, during the tumultuous years in store for mankind, and in this same domain, a commotion still more devastating than it has yet produced?

The dramatic collapse of both the Second Empire 135 and the Napoleonic dynasty, the virtual extinction of the temporal sovereignty of the Supreme Pontiff, in the lifetime of Bahá'u'lláh, were but the precursors of still greater catastrophes that may be said to have marked the ministry of 'Abdu'l-Bahá. The forces unleashed by a conflict, the full significance of which still remains unfathomed, and which may be considered as a prelude to this, the most devastating of all wars, can well be regarded as the occasion of these dreadful catastrophes. The progress of the War of 1914–18 dethroned the House of Romanov, while its termination precipitated the downfall of both the Hapsburg and Hohenzollern dynasties.

The Rise of Bolshevism

136 The rise of Bolshevism, born amidst the fires of that inconclusive struggle, shook the throne of the Czars and overthrew it. Alexander II Nicolaevich, whom Bahá'u'lláh had commanded in His Tablet to *"arise . . . and summon the nations unto God,"* who had been thrice warned: *"beware lest thy desire deter thee from turning towards the face of thy Lord,"* *"beware lest thou barter away this sublime station,"* *"beware lest thy sovereignty withhold thee from Him Who is the Supreme Sovereign,"* was not indeed the last of the Czars to rule his country, but rather the inaugurator of a retrogressive policy which in the end proved fatal to both himself and his dynasty.

137 In the latter part of his reign he initiated a reactionary policy which, causing widespread disillusion-

ment, gave rise to Nihilism, which, as it spread, ushered in a period of terrorism of unexampled violence,
leading in its turn to several attempts on his life, and
culminating in his assassination. Stern repression
guided the policy of his successor, Alexander III, who
"assumed an attitude of defiant hostility to innovators
and liberals." The tradition of unqualified absolutism,
of extreme religious orthodoxy was maintained by the
still more severe Nicolas II, the last of the Czars, who,
guided by the counsels of a man who was "the very
incarnation of a narrow-minded, stiff-necked despotism," and aided by a corrupt bureaucracy, and hu-
miliated by the disastrous effects of a foreign war, in-
creased the general discontent of the masses, both intellectuals and peasants. Driven for a time into subterranean channels, and intensified by military reverses,
it exploded at last in the midst of the Great War, in the
form of a Revolution which, in the principles it challenged, the institutions it subverted, and the havoc it
wrought, has scarcely a parallel in modern history.

A great trembling seized and rocked the founda-   138
tions of that country. The light of religion was dimmed.
Ecclesiastical institutions of every denomination were
swept away. The state religion was disendowed, persecuted, and abolished. A far-flung empire was dismem-
bered. A militant, triumphant proletariat exiled the
intellectuals, and plundered and massacred the nobil-
ity. Civil war and disease decimated a population, already in the throes of agony and despair. And, finally,

the Chief Magistrate of a mighty dominion, together with his consort, and his family, and his dynasty, were swept into the vortex of this great convulsion, and perished.

139   The very ordeal that heaped such dire misfortunes on the empire of the Czars brought about, in its concluding stages, the fall of the almighty German Kaiser as well as that of the inheritor of the once famed Holy Roman Empire. It shattered the whole fabric of Imperial Germany, which arose out of the disaster that engulfed the Napoleonic dynasty, and dealt the Dual Monarchy its death blow.

140   Almost half a century before, Bahá'u'lláh, Who had predicted, in clear and resounding terms, the ignominious fall of the successor of the great Napoleon, had, in the Kitáb-i-Aqdas, addressed to Kaiser William I, the newly acclaimed victor, a no less significant warning, and prophesied, in His apostrophe to the banks of the Rhine, in words equally unambiguous, the mourning that would afflict the capital of the newly federated empire.

141   "*Do thou remember,*" Bahá'u'lláh thus addressed him, "*the one* [Napoleon] *whose power transcended thy power, and whose station excelled thy station. . . . Think deeply, O king, concerning him, and concerning them who, like unto thee, have conquered cities and ruled over men.*" And again: "*O banks of the Rhine! We have seen you covered with gore, inasmuch as the swords of retribution were drawn against you; and you shall have another*

turn. And We hear the lamentations of Berlin, though she be today in conspicuous glory."

On him who, in his old age, sustained two attempts upon his life by the advocates of the rising tide of socialism; on his son Frederick III, whose three months' reign was overshadowed by mortal disease; and finally on his grandson, William II, the self-willed and overweening monarch and wrecker of his own empire—on these fell, in varying degrees, the full weight of the responsibilities consequent to these dire pronouncements. 142

William I, first German Emperor and seventh king of Prussia, whose entire lifetime had, up to the date of his accession, been spent in the army, was a militaristic, autocratic ruler, imbued with antiquated ideas, who initiated, with the aid of a statesman rightly regarded as "one of the geniuses of his century," a policy which may be said to have inaugurated a new era not only for Prussia but for the world. This policy was pursued with characteristic thoroughness and perfected through the repressive measures that were taken to safeguard and uphold it, through the wars that were waged for its realization, and the political combinations that were subsequently formed to exalt and consolidate it, combinations that were fraught with such dreadful consequences to the European continent. 143

William II, temperamentally dictatorial, politically inexperienced, militarily aggressive, religiously insincere, posed as the apostle of European peace, yet actu- 144 ally insisted on "the mailed fist" and "the shining armor." Irresponsible, indiscreet, inordinately ambitious, his first act was to dismiss that sagacious statesman, the true founder of his empire, to whose sagacity Bahá'u'lláh had paid tribute, and to the unwisdom of whose imperial and ungrateful master 'Abdu'l-Bahá had testified. War indeed became a religion of his country, and by enlarging the scope of his multifarious activities, he proceeded to prepare the way for that final catastrophe that was to dethrone him and his dynasty. And when the war broke out, and the might of his armies seemed to have overpowered his adversaries, and the news of his triumphs was noised abroad, reverberating as far as Persia, voices were raised ridiculing those passages of the Kitáb-i-Aqdas which so clearly foreshadowed the misfortunes that were to befall his capital. Suddenly, however, swift and unforeseen reverses fatally overtook him. Revolution broke out. William II, deserting his armies, fled ignominiously to Holland, followed by the Crown Prince. The princes of the German states abdicated. A period of chaos ensued. The communist flag was hoisted in the capital, which became a caldron of confusion and civil strife. The Kaiser signed his abdication. The Constitution of Weimar established the Republic, bringing the tremendous structure, so elaborately reared through a policy of blood and iron, crashing to the ground. All the efforts to that end, which through internal legislation and foreign wars had, ever since the accession of William I to the Prussian throne, been assiduously exerted, came to naught. *"The lamentations of Berlin,"* tortured by the terms of a treaty monstrous in its severity, were raised, contrasting with the hilarious shouts of victory that rang, half a century before, in the Hall of Mirrors of the Palace of Versailles.

The Hapsburg monarch, heir of centuries of glo- 145 rious history, simultaneously toppled from his throne. It was Francis Joseph, whom Bahá'u'lláh chided in the Kitáb-i-Aqdas for having failed in his duty to investigate His Cause, let alone to seek His presence, when so easily accessible to him in the course of his visit to the Holy Land. *"Thou passed Him by,"* He thus reproves the pilgrim-emperor, *"and inquired not about Him. . . . We have been with thee at all times, and found thee clinging unto the Branch and heedless of the Root. . . . Open thine eyes, that thou mayest behold this Glorious Vision and recognize Him Whom thou invokest in the daytime and in the night season, and gaze on the Light that shineth above this luminous Horizon."*

The House of Hapsburg, in which the Imperial 146 Title had remained practically hereditary for almost five centuries, was, ever since those words were uttered, being increasingly menaced by the forces of internal disintegration, and was sowing the seeds of an external conflict, to both of which it ultimately succumbed. Francis Joseph, Emperor of Austria, King of Hungary, a reactionary ruler, reestablished old abuses, ignored the rights of nationalities, and restored that bureaucratic centralization that proved in the end so injurious to his empire. Repeated tragedies darkened his reign. His brother Maximilian was shot in Mexico. The Crown Prince Rudolph perished in a dishonorable affair. The Empress was assassinated in Geneva. Archduke Francis Ferdinand and his wife were murdered in Sarajevo, kindling a war in the midst of which the Emperor himself died, closing a reign which is unsurpassed by any other reign in the disasters it brought to the nation.

End of the Holy Roman Empire

147 Belated efforts had been made to steady his tottering throne. The "ramshackle empire," a medley of states, races, and languages, was, however, relentlessly and rapidly disintegrating. The political and economic situation was desperate. The defeat of Austria and Hungary, in that same war, sounded its death knell and brought its dismemberment. Hungary sundered its connection. The conglomerate realm was carved up, and all that was left of the once formidable Holy Roman Empire was a shrunken republic that led a miserable existence until, in more recent times, it was, unlike its sister nation, completely extinguished and wiped off the political map of Europe.

148 Such was the fate of the Napoleonic, the Romanov, the Hohenzollern, and the Hapsburg empires, whose

rulers, together with the sovereign occupant of the
Papal throne, were individually addressed by the Pen
of the Most High, and who were respectively chas-
tised, forewarned, condemned, rebuked and admonished. What of the fate of those sovereigns who, exercising direct political jurisdiction over the Faith, its
Founders, and followers, and within the radius of
whose domains that Faith was born and first spread,
were at liberty to crucify its Herald, banish its Founder,
and mow down its adherents?

What of Turkey and Persia?

Already in the lifetime of Bahá'u'lláh, and later during 149
the ministry of 'Abdu'l-Bahá, the first blows of a slow
yet steady and relentless retribution were falling alike
upon the rulers of the Turkish House of 'U<u>th</u>mán and
of the Qájár dynasty in Persia—the archenemies of
God's infant Faith. Sulṭán 'Abdu'l-'Azíz fell from power,
and was murdered soon after Bahá'u'lláh's banishment
from Adrianople, while Náṣiri'd-Dín <u>Sh</u>áh succumbed
to an assassin's pistol, during 'Abdu'l-Bahá's incarceration in the fortress-town of 'Akká. It was reserved, however, for the Formative Period of the Faith of God—
the Age of the birth and rise of its Administrative Order—which, as stated in a previous communication,
is through its unfoldment casting such a turmoil in
the world, to witness not only the extinction of both

of these dynasties, but also the abolition of the twin institutions of the Sultanate and the Caliphate.

150   Of the two despots 'Abdu'l-'Azíz was the more powerful, the more exalted in rank, the more preeminent in guilt, and the more concerned with the tribulations and fortunes of the Founder of our Faith. He it was who, through his farmáns, had thrice banished Bahá'u'lláh, and in whose dominions the Manifestation of God spent almost the whole of His forty years' captivity. It was during his reign and that of his nephew and successor, 'Abdu'l-Ḥamíd II, that the Center of the Covenant of God had to endure, for no less than forty years, in the fortress-town of 'Akká, an incarceration fraught with so many perils, affronts and privations.

151   *"Hearken, O king!"* is the summons issued to Sulṭán 'Abdu'l-'Azíz by Bahá'u'lláh, *"to the speech of Him that speaketh the truth, Him that doth not ask thee to recompense Him with the things God hath chosen to bestow upon thee, Him Who unerringly treadeth the Straight Path. . . . Observe, O king, with thine inmost heart and with thy whole being, the precepts of God, and walk not in the paths of the oppressor. . . . Place not thy reliance on thy treasures. Put thy whole confidence in the grace of God, thy Lord. . . . Overstep not the bounds of moderation, and deal justly with them that serve thee. . . . Set before thine eyes God's unerring Balance, and, as one standing in His presence, weigh in that Balance thine actions, every day, every moment of thy life. Bring thyself*

to account ere thou art summoned to a reckoning, on the Day when no man shall have strength to stand for fear of God, the Day when the hearts of the heedless ones shall be made to tremble."

"*The day is approaching,*" Bahá'u'lláh thus proph-   152
esies in the Lawḥ-i-Ra'ís, "*when the Land of Mystery* [Adrianople], *and what is beside it shall be changed, and shall pass out of the hands of the king, and commotions shall appear, and the voice of lamentation shall be raised, and the evidences of mischief shall be revealed on all sides, and confusion shall spread by reason of that which hath befallen these captives at the hands of the hosts of oppression. The course of things shall be altered, and conditions shall wax so grievous, that the very sands on the desolate hills will moan, and the trees on the mountain will weep, and blood will flow out of all things. Then wilt thou behold the people in sore distress.*"

"*Soon,*" He, moreover has written, "*will He seize*   153
you in His wrathful anger, and sedition will be stirred up in your midst, and your dominions will be disrupted. Then will ye bewail and lament, and will find none to help or succor you. . . . Several times calamities have overtaken you, and yet ye failed utterly to take heed. One of them was the conflagration which devoured most of the City [Constantinople] *with the flames of justice, and concerning which many poems were written, stating that no such fire had ever been witnessed. And yet, ye waxed more heedless. . . . Plague, likewise, broke out, and ye still failed to give heed! Be expectant, however, for the*

wrath of God is ready to overtake you. Erelong will ye behold that which hath been sent down from the Pen of My command."

154   *"By your deeds,"* He, in another Tablet, anticipating the fall of the Sultanate and the Caliphate, thus reproves the combined forces of Sunní and <u>Sh</u>í'ih Islám, *"the exalted station of the people hath been abased, the standard of Islám hath been reversed, and its mighty throne hath fallen."*

155   And finally, in the Kitáb-i-Aqdas, revealed soon after Bahá'u'lláh's banishment to 'Akká, He thus apostrophizes the seat of Turkish imperial power: *"O Spot that art situate on the shores of the two seas! The throne of tyranny hath, verily, been stablished upon thee, and the flame of hatred hath been kindled within thy bosom. . . . Thou art indeed filled with manifest pride. Hath thine outward splendor made thee vainglorious? By Him Who is the Lord of mankind! It shall soon perish, and thy daughters, and thy widows, and all the kindreds that dwell within thee shall lament. Thus informeth thee, the All-Knowing, the All-Wise."*

156   Indeed, in a most remarkable passage in the Law<u>h</u>-i-Fu'ád, wherein mention has been made of the death of Fu'ád Pá<u>sh</u>á, the Turkish Minister of Foreign Affairs, the fall of the Sul<u>t</u>án himself is unmistakably foretold: *"Soon will We dismiss the one who was like unto him, and will lay hold on their Chief who ruleth the land, and I, verily, am the Almighty, the All-Compelling."*

157   The Sul<u>t</u>án's reaction to these words, bearing upon his person, his empire, his throne, his capital, and his

ministers, can be gathered from the recital of the
sufferings he inflicted on Bahá'u'lláh, and already referred to in the beginning of these pages. The extinction of the *"outward splendor"* surrounding that proud
seat of Imperial power is the theme I now proceed to
expose.

The Doom of Imperial Turkey

A cataclysmic process, one of the most remarkable in   158
modern history, was set in motion ever since Bahá'-
u'lláh, while a prisoner in Constantinople, delivered
to a Turkish official His Tablet, addressed to Sulṭán
'Abdu'l-'Azíz and his ministers, to be transmitted to
'Álí Páshá, the Grand Vizir. It was this Tablet which,
as attested by that officer and affirmed by Nabíl in his
chronicle, affected the Vizir so profoundly that he paled
while reading it. This process received fresh impetus
after the Lawḥ-i-Ra'ís was revealed on the morrow of
its Author's final banishment from Adrianople to 'Akká.
Relentless, devastating, and with ever-increasing momentum, it ominously unfolded, damaging the prestige of the Empire, dismembering its territory, dethron-
ing its sulṭáns, sweeping away their dynasty, degrad-
ing and deposing its Caliph, disestablishing its religion, and extinguishing its glory. The "sick man" of
Europe, whose condition had been unerringly diag-
nosed by the Divine Physician, and whose doom was
pronounced inevitable, fell a prey, during the reign of

five successive sulṭáns, all degenerate, all deposed, to a
series of convulsions which, in the end, proved fatal to
his life. Imperial Turkey that had, under 'Abdu'l-Majíd,
been admitted into the European Concert, and had
emerged victorious from the Crimean War, entered,
under his successor, 'Abdu'l-'Azíz, upon a period of
swift decline, culminating, soon after 'Abdu'l-Bahá's
passing, in the doom which the judgment of God had
pronounced against it.

159   Risings in Crete and the Balkans marked the reign
of this, the 32nd sulṭán of his dynasty, a despot whose
mind was vacuous, whose recklessness was extreme,
whose extravagance knew no bounds. The Eastern
Question entered upon an acute phase. His gross mis-
rule gave rise to movements which were to exercise
far-reaching effects upon his realm, while his continual
and enormous borrowings, leading to a state of semi-
bankruptcy, introduced the principle of foreign control over the finances of his empire. A conspiracy, leading to a palace revolution, finally deposed him. A fatvá
of the muftí denounced his incapacity and extravagance. Four days later he was assassinated, and was
succeeded by his nephew, Murád V, whose mind had
been reduced to a nullity by intemperance and by a
long seclusion in the Cage. Declared to be imbecile,
he, after a reign of three months, was deposed and was
succeeded by the subtle, the resourceful, the suspicious,
the tyrannical 'Abdu'l-Ḥamíd II who "proved to be
the most mean, cunning, untrustworthy and cruel in-

triguer of the long dynasty of 'U<u>th</u>mán." "No one knew," it was written of him, "from day to day who was the person on whose advice the sul<u>t</u>án overruled his ostensible ministers, whether a favorite lady of his harem, or a eunuch, or some fanatical dervish, or an astrologer, or a spy." The Bulgarian atrocities heralded the black reign of this "Great Assassin," which thrilled Europe with horror, and were characterized by Gladstone as "the basest and blackest outrages upon record in that [XIX] century." The War of 1877–78 accelerated the process of the empire's dismemberment. No less than eleven million people were emancipated from Turkish yoke. The Russian troops occupied Adrianople. Serbia, Montenegro and Rumania proclaimed their independence. Bulgaria became a self-governing state, tributary to the sul<u>t</u>án. Cyprus and Egypt were occupied. The French assumed a protectorate over Tunis. Eastern Rumelia was ceded to Bulgaria. The wholesale massacres of Armenians, involving directly and indirectly a hundred thousand souls, were but a foretaste of the still more extensive bloodbaths to come in a later reign. Bosnia and Herzegovina were lost to Austria. Bulgaria obtained her independence. Universal contempt and hatred of an infamous sovereign, shared alike by his Christian and Muslim subjects, finally culminated in a revolution, swift and sweeping. The Committee of Young Turks secured from the <u>Sh</u>ay<u>kh</u>u'l-Islám the condemnation of the sul<u>t</u>án. Deserted and friendless, execrated by his sub-

jects, and despised by his fellow-rulers, he was forced
to abdicate, and was made a prisoner of state, thus
ending a reign "more disastrous in its immediate losses
of territory and in the certainty of others to follow,
and more conspicuous for the deterioration of the condition of his subjects, than that of any other of his
twenty-three degenerate predecessors since the death
of Soliman the Magnificent."

160   The end of so shameful a reign was but the beginning of a new era which, however auspiciously hailed
at first, was destined to witness the collapse of the
Ottoman ramshackle and worm-eaten state. Muḥammad V, a brother of ʻAbdu'l-Ḥamíd II, an absolute non-
entity, failed to improve the status of his subjects. The
follies of his government ultimately sealed the doom
of the empire. The War of 1914–18 provided the occasion. Military reverses brought to a head the forces that
were sapping its foundations. While the war was still
being fought the defection of the Sherif of Mecca and
the revolt of the Arabian provinces portended the convulsion which was to seize the Turkish throne. The
precipitate flight and complete destruction of the army
of Jamál Páshá, the commander-in-chief in Syria—he
who had sworn to raze to the ground, after his triumphant return from Egypt, the Tomb of Baháʼuʼlláh,
and to publicly crucify the Center of His Covenant in
a public square of Constantinople—was the signal for
the nemesis that was to overtake an empire in distress.
Nine-tenths of the large Turkish armies had melted

away. A fourth of the whole population had perished from war, disease, famine and massacre.

A new ruler, Muḥammad VI, the last of the 161 twenty-five successive degenerate sulṭáns, had meanwhile succeeded his wretched brother. The edifice of the empire was now quaking and tottering to its fall. Muṣṭafá Kamál dealt it the final blows. Turkey, that had already shrunk to a small Asiatic state, became a republic. The sulṭán was deposed, the Ottoman Sultanate was ended, a rulership that had remained unbroken for six and a half centuries was extinguished. An empire which had stretched from the center of Hungary to the Persian Gulf and the Sudan, and from the Caspian Sea to Oran in Africa, had now dwindled to a small Asiatic republic. Constantinople itself, which, after the fall of Byzantium, had been honored as the splendid metropolis of the Roman Empire, and had been made the capital of the Ottoman government, was abandoned by its conquerors, and stripped of its pomp and glory—a mute reminder of the base tyranny that had for so long stained its throne.

Such, in their bare outline, were the awful evi- 162 dences of that retributive justice which so tragically afflicted ‘Abdu’l-‘Azíz, his successors, his throne and his dynasty. What of Náṣiri’d-Dín Sháh, the other partner in that imperial conspiracy which sought to extirpate, root and branch, the budding Faith of God? His reaction to the Divine Message borne to him by the fearless Badí‘, the "Pride of Martyrs," who had spontaneously dedicated himself to this purpose, was characteristic of that implacable hatred which, throughout his reign, glowed so fiercely in his breast.

Divine Retribution on the Qájár Dynasty

163   The French Emperor had, it was reported, flung away Bahá'u'lláh's Tablet, and directed his minister, as Bahá'u'lláh Himself asserts, to address to its Author an irreverent reply. The Grand Vizir of 'Abdu'l-'Azíz, it is reliably stated, blanched while reading the communication addressed to his Imperial master and his ministers, and made the following comment: "It is as if the king of kings were issuing his behest to his humblest vassal king, and regulating his conduct!" Queen Victoria, it is said, upon reading the Tablet revealed for her remarked: "If this is of God, it will endure; if not, it can do no harm." It was reserved for Násiri'd-Dín Sháh, however, to wreak, at the instigation of the divines, his vengeance on One Whom he could no longer personally chastise by arresting His messenger, a lad of about seventeen, by freighting him with chains, by torturing him on the rack, and finally slaying him.

164   To this despotic sovereign Bahá'u'lláh, Who denounced him as the *"Prince of Oppressors,"* and as one who would soon be made *"an object-lesson for the world,"* had written: *"Look upon this Youth, O king, with the eyes of justice; judge thou, then, with truth concerning*

what hath befallen Him. Of a verity, God hath made thee His shadow amongst men, and the sign of His power unto all that dwell on earth." And again: *"O king! Wert thou to incline thine ears unto the shrill of the Pen of Glory and the cooing of the Dove of Eternity . . . thou wouldst attain unto a station from which thou wouldst behold in the world of being naught save the effulgence of the Adored One, and wouldst regard thy sovereignty as the most contemptible of thy possessions, abandoning it to whosoever might desire it, and setting thy face toward the horizon aglow with the light of His countenance."* And again: *"We fain would hope, however, that His Majesty the Sháh will himself examine these matters, and bring hope to the hearts. That which We have submitted to thee is indeed for thine highest good."*

This hope, however, was to remain unfulfilled. It 165 was indeed shattered by a reign which had been inaugurated by the execution of the Báb, and the imprisonment of Bahá'u'lláh in the Síyáh-Chál of Ṭihrán, by a sovereign who had repeatedly instigated Bahá'u'lláh's successive banishments, and by a dynasty that had been sullied by the slaughter of no less than twenty thousand of His followers. The Sháh's dramatic assassination, the ignoble rule of the last sovereigns of the House of Qájár, and the extinction of that dynasty, were signal instances of the Divine retribution which these horrid atrocities had provoked.

The Qájárs, members of the alien Turkoman tribe, 166 had, indeed, usurped the Persian throne. Áqá Muḥam-

mad <u>Kh</u>án, the eunuch <u>Sh</u>áh and founder of the dynasty, was such an atrocious, avaricious, blood-thirsty
tyrant that the memory of no Persian is so detested
and universally execrated as his memory. The record
of his reign and that of his immediate successors is one
of vandalism, of internal warfare, of recalcitrant and
rebellious chieftains, of brigandage, and medieval oppression, whilst the annals of the reigns of the later
Qájárs are marked by the stagnation of the nation, the
illiteracy of the people, the corruption and incompe-
tence of the government, the scandalous intrigues of
the court, the decadence of the princes, the irrespon-
sibility and extravagance of the sovereign, and his abject subservience to a notoriously degraded clerical order.

167   The successor of Áqá Mu<u>h</u>ammad <u>Kh</u>án, the uxo-
rious, philoprogenetive Fat<u>h</u>-'Alí <u>Sh</u>áh, the so-called
"Darius of the Age," was a vain, an arrogant, and un-
scrupulous miser, notorious for the enormous number
of his wives and concubines, numbering above a thousand, his incalculable progeny, and the disasters which
his rule brought upon his country. He it was who commanded that his vizir, to whom he owed his throne,
be cast into a caldron of boiling oil. As to his successor, the bigoted Mu<u>h</u>ammad <u>Sh</u>áh, one of his earliest
acts, definitely condemned by the pen of Bahá'u'lláh,
was the order to strangle his first minister, the illustri-
ous Qá'im-Maqám, immortalized by that same pen as
the *"Prince of the City of Statesmanship and Literary*

Accomplishment," and to have him replaced by that lowbred, consummate scoundrel, Ḥájí Mírzá Áqásí, who brought the country to the verge of bankruptcy and revolution. It was this same Sẖáh who refused to interview the Báb and imprisoned Him in Ádẖirbáyján, and who, at the age of forty, was afflicted by a complication of maladies to which he succumbed, hastening the doom forecast in these words of the Qayyúm-i-Asmá': *"I swear by God, O Sẖáh! If thou showest enmity unto Him Who is His Remembrance, God will, on the Day of Resurrection, condemn thee, before the kings, unto hellfire, and thou shalt not, in very truth, find on that day any helper except God, the Exalted."*

Náṣiri'd-Dín Sẖáh, a selfish, capricious, imperious monarch, succeeded to the throne, and, for half a century, was destined to remain the sole arbiter of the fortunes of his hapless country. A disastrous obscurantism, a chaotic administration in the provinces, the disorganization of the finances of the realm, the intrigues, the vindictiveness, and profligacy of the pampered and greedy courtiers, who buzzed and swarmed round his throne, his own despotism which, but for the restraining fear of European public opinion and the desire to be thought well of in the capitals of the West, would have been more cruel and savage, were the distinguishing features of the bloody reign of one who styled himself "Footpath of Heaven," and "Asylum of the Universe." A triple darkness of chaos, bankruptcy and oppression enveloped the country. His own

168

assassination was the first portent of the revolution which was to restrict the prerogatives of his son and successor, depose the last two monarchs of the House of Qájár, and extinguish their dynasty. On the eve of his jubilee, which was to inaugurate a new era, and the celebration of which had been elaborately prepared, he fell, in the shrine of Sháh 'Abdu'l-'Azím, a victim to an assassin's pistol, his dead body driven back to his capitol, propped up in the royal carriage in front of his Grand Vizir, in order to defer the news of his murder.

169   "It was whispered," writes an eyewitness of both the ceremony and the assassination, "that the day of the Sháh's celebration was to be the greatest in the history of Persia. . . . Prisoners were to be released without condition, and a general amnesty was to be proclaimed; peasants were promised exemption from taxes for at least two years. . . . the poor were to be fed for months. Ministers and officials were already intriguing for honors and pension from the Sháh. Shrines and sacred places were to open their gates to all wayfarers and pilgrims, and the siyyids and mullás were taking cough medicine to clear their throats to sing and chant the praises of the Sháh in all the pulpits. The mosques were swept and prepared for general meetings and public prayers in behalf of the Sovereign. . . . Sacred fountains were enlarged to hold more holy water, and the rightful authorities had foreseen that many miracles might take place on the day of the

jubilee, with the aid of these fountains. . . . The <u>Sh</u>áh had declared . . . that he would renounce his prerogatives as despot, and proclaim himself 'The Majestic Father of all the Persians.' The city authority was to relax its vigilant watch. No record was to be kept of the strangers who flocked to the caravanserais, and the population was to be left free to wander the streets during the whole night." Even the great mujtahids had, according to what had been reported to that same eyewitness, "decided, for the time being, to discontinue persecuting the Bábís and other infidels."

Thus fell the one whose reign will remain forever   170 associated with the most heinous crime in history— the martyrdom of that One Whom the Supreme Manifestation of God proclaimed to be the *"Point round Whom the realities of the Prophets and Messengers revolve."* In a Tablet in which the pen of Bahá'u'lláh condemns him, we read: *"Among them* [kings of the earth] *is the King of Persia, who suspended Him Who is the Temple of the Cause* [the Báb] *in the air, and put Him to death with such cruelty that all created things, and the inmates of Paradise, and the Concourse on high wept for Him. He slew, moreover, some of Our kindred, and plundered Our property, and made Our family captives in the hands of the oppressors. Once and again he imprisoned Me. By God, the True One! None can reckon the things which befell Me in prison, save God, the Reckoner, the Omniscient, the Almighty. Subsequently he banished Me and My family from My country, whereupon We arrived in 'Iráq in evi-*

dent sorrow. We tarried there until the time when the King of Rúm [Sulṭán of Turkey] *arose against Us, and summoned Us unto the seat of his sovereignty. When We reached it there flowed over Us that whereat the King of Persia rejoiced. Later We entered this Prison, wherein the hands of Our loved ones were torn from the hem of Our robe. In such a manner hath he dealt with Us!"*

171   The days of the Qájár dynasty were now numbered. The torpor of the national consciousness had vanished. The reign of Náṣiri'd-Dín Sháh's successor, Muẓaffari'd-Dín Sháh, a weak and timid creature, extravagant and lavish to his courtiers, led the country down the broad road to ruin. The movement in favor of a constitution, limiting the sovereign's prerogatives, gathered force, and culminated in the signature of the constitution by the dying Sháh, who expired a few days later. Muḥammad-'Alí Sháh, a despot of the worst type, unprincipled and avaricious, succeeded to the throne. Hostile to the constitution, he, by his summary action, involving the bombardment of the Baháristán, where the Assembly met, precipitated a revolution which led to his deposition by the nationalists. Accepting, after much bargaining, a large pension, he ignominiously withdrew to Russia. The boy-king, Aḥmad Sháh, who succeeded him, was a mere cipher and careless of his duties. The crying needs of his country continued to be ignored. Increasing anarchy, the impotence of the central government, the state of the national finances, the progressive deterioration of the general condition of the country, practically

abandoned by a sovereign who preferred the gaieties and frivolities of society life in the European capitals to the discharge of the stern and urgent responsibilities which the plight of his nation demanded, sounded the death knell of a dynasty which, it was generally felt, had forfeited the crown. Whilst abroad, on one of his periodic visits, Parliament deposed him, and proclaimed the extinction of his dynasty, which had occupied the throne of Persia for a hundred and thirty years, whose rulers proudly claimed no less a descent than from Japhet, son of Noah, and whose successive monarchs, with only one exception, were either assassinated, deposed, or struck down by a mortal disease.

Their myriad progeny, a veritable "beehive of 172 princelings," a "race of royal drones," were both a disgrace and a menace to their countrymen. Now, however, these luckless descendants of a fallen house, shorn of all power, and some of them reduced even to beggary, proclaim, in their distress, the consequences of the abominations which their progenitors have perpetrated. Swelling the ranks of the ill-fated scions of the House of 'Uthmán, and of the rulers of the Romanov, the Hohenzollern, the Hapsburg, and the Napoleonic dynasties, they roam the face of the earth, scarcely aware of the character of those forces which have operated such tragic revolutions in their lives, and so powerfully contributed to their present plight.

Already grandsons of both Náṣiri'd-Dín Sháh and 173 of Sulṭán 'Abdu'l-'Azíz have, in their powerlessness and destitution, turned to the World Center of the Faith of Bahá'u'lláh, and sought respectively political aid and pecuniary assistance. In the case of the former, the request was promptly and firmly refused, whilst in the case of the latter it was unhesitatingly offered.

The Decline in
the Fortunes of Royalty

174   And as we survey in other fields the decline in the fortunes of royalty, whether in the years immediately preceding the Great War or after, and contemplate the fate that has overtaken the Chinese Empire, the Portuguese and Spanish Monarchies, and more recently the vicissitudes that have afflicted, and are still afflicting, the sovereigns of Norway, of Denmark and of Holland, and observe the impotence of their fellow-sovereigns, and note the fear and trembling that has seized their thrones, may we not associate their plight with the opening passages of the Súriy-i-Mulúk, which, in view of their momentous significance, I feel impelled to quote a second time: *"Fear God, O concourse of kings, and suffer not yourselves to be deprived of this most sublime grace. . . . Set your hearts towards the face of God, and abandon that which your desires have bidden you to follow, and be not of those who perish. . . . Ye examined not His* [the Báb's] *Cause, when so to do had been better for you than all that the sun shineth upon, could ye but perceive it. . . . Beware that ye be not careless hence-*

forth, as ye have been careless aforetime. . . . My face hath come forth from the veils, and shed its radiance upon all that is in heaven and on earth, and yet ye turned not towards Him. . . . Arise then . . . and make ye amends for that which hath escaped you. . . . If ye pay no heed unto the counsels which, in peerless and unequivocal language, We have revealed in this Tablet, Divine chastisement shall assail you from every direction, and the sentence of His justice shall be pronounced against you. . . . Twenty years have passed, O kings, during which We have, each day, tasted the agony of a fresh tribulation. . . . Though aware of most of Our afflictions, ye, nevertheless, have failed to stay the hand of the aggressor. For is it not your clear duty to restrain the tyranny of the oppressor, and to deal equitably with your subjects, that your high sense of justice may be fully demonstrated to all mankind?"

No wonder that Bahá'u'lláh, in view of the treatment meted out to Him by the sovereigns of the earth, should, as already quoted, have written these words: *"From two ranks amongst men power hath been seized: kings and ecclesiastics."* Indeed, He even goes further, and states in His Tablet addressed to <u>Shaykh</u> Salmán: *"One of the signs of the maturity of the world is that no one will accept to bear the weight of kingship. Kingship will remain with none willing to bear alone its weight. That day will be the day whereon wisdom will be manifested among mankind. Only in order to proclaim the Cause of God and spread abroad His Faith will anyone be* 175

*willing to bear this grievous weight. Well is it with him
who, for the love of God and His Cause, and for the sake
of God and for the purpose of proclaiming His Faith, will
expose himself unto this great danger, and will accept this
toil and trouble."*

Recognition of Kingship

176 Let none, however, mistake or unwittingly misrepresent the purpose of Bahá'u'lláh. Severe as has been His
condemnation pronounced against those sovereigns
who persecuted Him, and however strict the censure
expressed collectively against those who failed signally
in their clear duty to investigate the truth of His Faith
and to restrain the hand of the wrongdoer, His teachings embody no principle that can, in any way, be construed as a repudiation, or even a disparagement, however veiled, of the institution of kingship. The catastrophic fall, and the extinction of the dynasties and
empires of those monarchs whose disastrous end He
particularly prophesied, and the declining fortunes of
the sovereigns of His Own generation, whom He generally reproved—both constituting a passing phase of
the evolution of the Faith—should, in no wise, be confounded with the future position of that institution.
Indeed if we delve into the writings of the Author of
the Bahá'í Faith, we cannot fail to discover unnumbered passages in which, in terms that none can mis-

represent, the principle of kingship is eulogized, the rank and conduct of just and fair-minded kings is extolled, the rise of monarchs, ruling with justice and even professing His Faith, is envisaged, and the solemn duty to arise and ensure the triumph of Bahá'í sovereigns is inculcated. To conclude from the above quoted words, addressed by Bahá'u'lláh to the monarchs of the earth, to infer from the recital of the woeful disasters that have overtaken so many of them, that His followers either advocate or anticipate the definite extinction of the institution of kingship, would indeed be tantamount to a distortion of His teaching.

I can do no better than quote some of Bahá'u'lláh's 177 Own testimonies, leaving the reader to shape his own judgment as to the falsity of such a deduction. In His "Epistle to the Son of the Wolf" He indicates the true source of kingship: *"Regard for the rank of sovereigns is divinely ordained, as is clearly attested by the words of the Prophets of God and His chosen ones. He Who is the Spirit* [Jesus] *—may peace be upon Him—was asked: 'O Spirit of God! Is it lawful to give tribute to Caesar, or not?' And He made reply: 'Yea, render to Caesar the things that are Caesar's, and to God the things that are God's.' He forbade it not. These two sayings are, in the estimation of men of insight, one and the same, for if that which belonged to Caesar had not come from God He would have forbidden it. And likewise in the sacred verse: 'Obey God and obey the Apostle, and those among you invested with authority.' By 'those invested with authority' is meant primarily*

*and more specially the Imáms—the blessings of God rest
upon them. They verily are the manifestations of the power
of God and the sources of His authority, and the repositories of His knowledge, and the daysprings of His commandments. Secondarily these words refer unto the kings
and rulers—those through the brightness of whose justice
the horizons of the world are resplendent and luminous."*

178   And again: *"In the Epistle to the Romans Saint Paul
hath written: 'Let every soul be subject unto the higher
powers. For there is no power but of God; the powers that
be are ordained of God. Whosoever, therefore, resisteth the
power, resisteth the ordinance of God.'"* And further: *"'For
he is the minister of God, a revenger to execute wrath
upon him that doeth evil.' He saith that the appearance of
the kings, and their majesty and power, are of God."*

179   And again: *"A just king enjoyeth nearer access unto
God than anyone. Unto this testifieth He Who speaketh in
His Most Great Prison."*

180   Likewise in the Bishárát (Glad-Tidings) Bahá'u'lláh
asserts that *"the majesty of kingship is one of the signs of
God."* *"We do not wish,"* He adds, *"that the countries of
the world should be deprived thereof."*

181   In the Kitáb-i-Aqdas He sets forth His purpose,
and eulogizes the king who will profess His Faith: *"By
the Righteousness of God! It is not Our wish to lay hands
on your kingdoms. Our mission is to seize and possess the
hearts of men. Upon them the eyes of Bahá are fastened.
To this testifieth the Kingdom of Names, could ye but comprehend it. Whoso followeth his Lord, will renounce the*

world and all that is therein; how much greater, then, must be the detachment of Him Who holdeth so august a station!" "How great the blessedness that awaiteth the king who will arise to aid My Cause in My Kingdom, who will detach himself from all else but Me! Such a king is numbered with the Companions of the Crimson Ark—the Ark which God hath prepared for the people of Bahá. All must glorify his name, must reverence his station, and aid him to unlock the cities with the keys of My Name, the Omnipotent Protector of all that inhabit the visible and invisible kingdoms. Such a king is the very eye of mankind, the luminous ornament on the brow of creation, the fountainhead of blessings unto the whole world. Offer up, O people of Bahá, your substance, nay your very lives, for his assistance."

In the Lawḥ-i-Sulṭán Bahá'u'lláh further reveals 182 the significance of kingship: *"A just king is the shadow of God on earth. All should seek shelter under the shadow of his justice, and rest in the shade of his favor. This is not a matter which is either specific or limited in its scope, that it might be restricted to one or another person, inasmuch as the shadow telleth of the One Who casteth it. God, glorified be His remembrance, hath called Himself the Lord of the worlds, for He hath nurtured and still nurtureth everyone. Glorified be, then, His grace that hath preceded all created things, and His mercy that hath surpassed the worlds."*

In one of His Tablets Bahá'u'lláh has also written: 183 *"The one true God, exalted be His glory, hath bestowed the government of the earth upon the kings. To none is given the right to act in any manner that would run counter to the considered views of them who are in authority. That which He hath reserved for Himself are the cities of men's hearts; and of these the loved ones of Him Who is the Sovereign Truth are, in this Day, as the keys."*

184   In the following passage He expresses this wish: *"We cherish the hope that one of the kings of the earth will, for the sake of God, arise for the triumph of this wronged, this oppressed people. Such a king will be eternally extolled and glorified. God hath prescribed unto this people the duty of aiding whosoever will aid them, of serving his best interests, and of demonstrating to him their abiding loyalty."*

185   In the Lawḥ-i-Ra'ís He actually and categorically prophesies the rise of such a king: *"Erelong will God raise up from among the kings one who will aid His loved ones. He, verily, encompasseth all things. He will instill in the hearts the love of His loved ones. This, indeed, is irrevocably decreed by One Who is the Almighty, the Beneficent."* In the Riḍván-u'l-'Adl, wherein the virtue of justice is exalted, He makes a parallel prediction: *"Erelong will God make manifest on earth kings who will recline on the couches of justice, and will rule amongst men even as they rule their own selves. They, indeed, are among the choicest of My creatures in the entire creation."*

186   In the Kitáb-i-Aqdas He visualizes in these words the elevation to the throne of His native city, *"the Mother of the World"* and *"the Dayspring of Light,"* of a king

who will be adorned with the twin ornaments of justice and of devotion to His Faith: *"Let nothing grieve thee, O Land of Ṭá, for God hath chosen thee to be the source of the joy of all mankind. He shall, if it be His will, bless thy throne with one who will rule with justice, who will gather together the flock of God which the wolves have scattered. Such a ruler will, with joy and gladness, turn his face towards and extend his favors unto, the people of Bahá. He indeed is accounted in the sight of God as a jewel among men. Upon him rest forever the glory of God, and the glory of all that dwell in the kingdom of His Revelation."*

The Crumbling of Religious Orthodoxy

Dear friends! The decline in the fortunes of the crowned 187 wielders of temporal power has been paralleled by a no less startling deterioration in the influence exercised by the world's spiritual leaders. The colossal events that have heralded the dissolution of so many kingdoms and empires have almost synchronized with the crumbling of the seemingly inviolable strongholds of religious orthodoxy. That same process which, swiftly and tragically, sealed the doom of kings and emperors, and extinguished their dynasties, has operated in the case of the ecclesiastical leaders of both Christianity and Islám, damaging their prestige, and, in some cases, overthrowing their highest institutions. *"Power hath been seized"* indeed from both *"kings and ecclesiastics."* The glory of the former has been eclipsed, the power of the latter irretrievably lost.

188   Those leaders who exercised guidance and control over the ecclesiastical hierarchies of their respective religions have, likewise, been appealed to, warned, and reproved by Bahá'u'lláh, in terms no less certain than those in which the sovereigns who presided over the destinies of their subjects have been addressed. They, too, and more particularly the heads of Muslim ecclesiastical orders, have, in conjunction with despots and potentates, launched their assaults and thundered their anathemas against the Founders of the Faith of God, its followers, its principles, and its institutions. Were not the divines of Persia the first who hoisted the standard of revolt, who inflamed the ignorant and subservient masses against it, and who instigated the civil authorities, through their outcry, their threats, their lies, their calumnies, and denunciations, to decree the banishments, to enact the laws, to launch the punitive campaigns, and to carry out the executions and massacres that fill the pages of its history? So abominable and savage was the butchery committed in a single day, instigated by these divines, and so typical of the "callousness of the brute and the ingenuity of the fiend" that Renan, in his "Les Apôtres," characterized that day as "perhaps unparalleled in the history of the world."

It was these divines, who, by these very acts, sowed   189
the seeds of the disintegration of their own institutions, institutions that were so potent, so famous, and
appeared so invulnerable when the Faith was born. It
was they who, by assuming so lightly and foolishly,
such awful responsibilities were primarily answerable
for the release of those violent and disruptive influ-
ences that have unchained disasters as catastrophic as
those which overwhelmed kings, dynasties, and empires, and which constitute the most noteworthy land-
marks in the history of the first century of the Bahá'í
era.

This process of deterioration, however startling in   190
its initial manifestations, is still operating with undi-
minished force, and will, as the opposition to the Faith
of God, from various sources and in distant fields,
gathers momentum, be further accelerated and reveal
still more remarkable evidences of its devastating power.
I cannot, in view of the proportions which this communication has already assumed, expatiate, as fully as
I would wish, on the aspects of this weighty theme
which, together with the reaction of the sovereigns of
the earth to the Message of Bahá'u'lláh, is one of the
most fascinating and edifying episodes in the dramatic
story of His Faith. I will only consider the repercussions of the violent assaults made by the ecclesiastical
leaders of Islám and, to a lesser degree, by certain exponents of Christian orthodoxy upon their respective
institutions. I will preface these observations with some

passages gleaned from the great mass of Bahá'u'lláh's Tablets which, both directly and indirectly, bear reference to Muslim and Christian divines, and which throw such a powerful light on the dismal disasters that have overtaken, and are still overtaking, the ecclesiastical hierarchies of the two religions with which the Faith has been immediately concerned.

191   It must not be inferred, however, that Bahá'u'lláh directed His historic addresses exclusively to the leaders of Islám and Christianity, or that the impact of an all-pervading Faith on the strongholds of religious orthodoxy is to be confined to the institutions of these two religious systems. *"The time foreordained unto the peoples and kindreds of the earth,"* affirms Bahá'u'lláh, *"is now come. The promises of God, as recorded in the Holy Scriptures, have all been fulfilled. . . . This is the Day which the Pen of the Most High hath glorified in all the Holy Scriptures. There is no verse in them that doth not declare the glory of His holy Name, and no Book that doth not testify unto the loftiness of this most exalted theme."* *"Were We,"* He adds, *"to make mention of all that hath been revealed in these heavenly Books and Holy Scriptures concerning this Revelation, this Tablet would assume impossible dimensions."* As the promise of the Faith of Bahá'u'lláh is enshrined in all the Scriptures of past religions, so does its Author address Himself to their followers, and particularly to their responsible leaders who have intervened between Him and their respective congregations. *"At one time,"* writes Bahá-

u'lláh, "*We address the people of the Torah and summon them unto Him Who is the Revealer of verses, Who hath come from Him Who layeth low the necks of men. . . . At another, We address the people of the Evangel and say: 'The All-Glorious is come in this Name whereby the Breeze of God hath wafted over all regions.' . . . At still another, We address the people of the Qur'án saying: 'Fear the All-Merciful, and cavil not at Him through Whom all religions were founded.' . . . Know thou, moreover, that We have addressed to the Magians Our Tablets, and adorned them with Our Law. . . . We have revealed in them the essence of all the hints and allusions contained in their Books. The Lord, verily, is the Almighty, the All-Knowing.*"

Addressing the Jewish people Bahá'u'lláh has written: "*The Most Great Law is come, and the Ancient Beauty ruleth upon the throne of David. Thus hath My Pen spoken that which the histories of bygone ages have related. At this time, however, David crieth aloud and saith: 'O my loving Lord! Do Thou number me with such as have stood steadfast in Thy Cause, O Thou through Whom the faces have been illumined, and the footsteps have slipped!'*" And again: "*The Breath hath been wafted, and the Breeze hath blown, and from Zion hath appeared that which was hidden, and from Jerusalem is heard the Voice of God, the One, the Incomparable, the Omniscient.*" Furthermore, in His "Epistle to the Son of the Wolf" Bahá'u'lláh has revealed: "*Lend an ear unto the song of David. He saith: 'Who will bring me into the Strong*

City?' The Strong City is 'Akká, which hath been named the Most Great Prison, and which possesseth a fortress and mighty ramparts. O _Shaykh!_ Peruse that which Isaiah hath spoken in His Book. He saith: 'Get thee up into the high mountain, O Zion, that bringest good tidings; lift up thy voice with strength, O Jerusalem, that bringest good tidings. Lift it up, be not afraid; say unto the cities of Judah: "Behold your God! Behold the Lord God will come with strong hand, and His arm shall rule for Him."' This Day all the signs have appeared. A Great City hath descended from heaven, and Zion trembleth and exulteth with joy at the Revelation of God, for it hath heard the Voice of God on every side."

193   To the priestly caste, holding sacerdotal supremacy over the followers of the Faith of Zoroaster, that same Voice, identifying itself with the voice of the promised _Sh_áh-Bahrám, has declared: "O high priests! Ears have been given you that they may hearken unto the mystery of Him Who is the Self-Dependent, and eyes that they may behold Him. Wherefore flee ye? The Incomparable Friend is manifest. He speaketh that wherein lieth salvation. Were ye, O high priests, to discover the perfume of the rose garden of understanding, ye would seek none other but Him, and would recognize, in His new vesture, the All-Wise and Peerless One, and would turn your eyes from the world and all who seek it, and would arise to help Him." "Whatsoever hath been announced in the Books," Bahá'u'lláh, replying to a Zoroastrian who had inquired regarding the promised _Sh_áh-Bahrám, has written, "hath been

revealed and made clear. From every direction the signs
have been manifested. The Omnipotent One is calling,
in this Day, and announcing the appearance of the Supreme Heaven." "This is not the day," He, in another
Tablet declares, "whereon the high priests can command
and exercise their authority. In your Book it is stated that
the high priests will, on that Day, lead men far astray,
and will prevent them from drawing nigh unto Him. He
indeed is a high priest who hath seen the light and has-
tened unto the way leading to the Beloved." "Say, O high
priests!" He, again addresses them, "The Hand of Om-
nipotence is stretched forth from behind the clouds; behold ye it with new eyes. The tokens of His majesty and
greatness are unveiled; gaze ye on them with pure
eyes. . . . Say, O high priests! Ye are held in reverence
because of My Name, and yet ye flee Me! Ye are the high
priests of the Temple. Had ye been the high priests of the
Omnipotent One, ye would have been united with Him,
and would have recognized Him. . . . Say, O high
priests! No man's acts shall be acceptable, in this Day,
unless he forsaketh mankind and all that men possess, and
setteth his face towards the Omnipotent One."

It is not, however, with either of these two Faiths 194
that we are primarily concerned. It is to Islám and, to
a lesser extent, to Christianity that my theme is directly related. Islám, from which the Faith of Bahá'-
u'lláh has sprung, even as did Christianity from Judaism, is the religion within whose pale that Faith first
rose and developed, from whose ranks the great mass

of Bahá'í adherents have been recruited, and by whose leaders they have been, and indeed are still being, persecuted. Christianity, on the other hand, is the religion to which the vast majority of Bahá'ís of non-Islamic extraction belong, within whose spiritual domain the Administrative Order of the Faith of God is rapidly advancing, and by whose ecclesiastical exponents that Order is being increasingly assailed. Unlike Hinduism, Buddhism, Judaism and even Zoroastrianism which, in the main, are still unaware of the potentialities of the Cause of God, and whose response to its Message is as yet negligible, the Muḥammadan and Christian Faiths may be regarded as the two religious systems which are sustaining, at this formative stage in its evolution, the full impact of so tremendous a Revelation.

195   Let us, then, consider what the Founders of the Bahá'í Faith have addressed to, or written about, the recognized leaders of Islám and Christianity. We have already considered the passages with reference to the kings of Islám, whether as Caliphs reigning in Constantinople, or as Sháhs of Persia who ruled the kingdom as temporary trustees for the expected Imám. We have also noted the Tablet which Bahá'u'lláh specifically revealed for the Roman Pontiff, and the more general message in the Súriy-i-Mulúk directed to the kings of Christendom. No less challenging and ominous is the Voice that has warned and called to account the Muḥammadan divines and the Christian clergy.

"*Leaders of religion,*" is Bahá'u'lláh's clear and uni- 196
versal censure pronounced in the Kitáb-i-Íqán, "*in every age, have hindered their people from attaining the
shores of eternal salvation, inasmuch as they held the reins
of authority in their mighty grasp. Some for the lust of
leadership, others through want of knowledge and understanding, have been the cause of the deprivation of the
people. By their sanction and authority, every Prophet of
God hath drunk from the chalice of sacrifice, and winged
His flight unto the heights of glory. What unspeakable
cruelties they that have occupied the seats of authority and
learning have inflicted upon the true Monarchs of the
world, those Gems of Divine virtue! Content with a tran-
sitory dominion, they have deprived themselves of an everlasting sovereignty.*" And again, in that same Book:
"*Among these 'veils of glory' are the divines and doctors
living in the days of the Manifestation of God, who, because of their want of discernment and their love and
eagerness for leadership, have failed to submit to the Cause
of God, nay, have even refused to incline their ears unto
the Divine Melody. 'They have thrust their fingers into
their ears.' And the people also, utterly ignoring God and
taking them for their masters, have placed themselves unreservedly under the authority of these pompous and hypocritical leaders, for they have no sight, no hearing, no
heart, of their own to distinguish truth from falsehood.
Notwithstanding the divinely inspired admonitions of all
the Prophets, the Saints, and Chosen Ones of God, en-
joining the people to see with their own eyes and hear*

with their own ears, they have disdainfully rejected their counsels and have blindly followed, and will continue to follow, the leaders of their Faith. Should a poor and obscure person, destitute of the attire of the men of learning, address them saying: 'Follow ye, O people, the Messengers of God,' they would, greatly surprised at such a statement, reply: 'What! Meanest thou that all these divines, all these exponents of learning, with all their authority, their pomp, and pageantry, have erred, and failed to distinguish truth from falsehood? Dost thou, and people like thyself, pretend to have comprehended that which they have not understood?' If numbers and excellence of apparel be regarded as the criterions of learning and truth, the peoples of a bygone age, whom those of today have never surpassed in numbers, magnificence and power, should certainly be accounted a superior and worthier people." Furthermore, *"Not one Prophet of God was made manifest Who did not fall a victim to the relentless hate, to the denunciation, denial and execration of the clerics of His day! Woe unto them for the iniquities their hands have formerly wrought! Woe unto them for that which they are now doing! What veils of glory more grievous than these embodiments of error! By the righteousness of God! To pierce such veils is the mightiest of all acts, and to rend them asunder the most meritorious of all deeds!"* *"On their tongue,"* He moreover has written, *"the mention of God hath become an empty name; in their midst His holy Word a dead letter. Such is the sway of their desires, that the lamp of conscience and reason hath been quenched in their hearts. . . . No two are found to agree on one and the same law, for they seek no God but their own desire, and tread no path but the path of error. In leadership they have recognized the ultimate object of their endeavor, and account pride and haughtiness as the highest attainments of their hearts' desire. They have placed their sordid machinations above the Divine decree, have renounced resignation unto the will of God, busied themselves with selfish calculation, and walked in the way of the hypocrite. With all their power and strength they strive to secure themselves in their petty pursuits, fearful lest the least discredit undermine their authority or blemish the display of their magnificence."*

"*The source and origin of tyranny,*" Bahá'u'lláh in 197 another Tablet has affirmed, "*have been the divines. Through the sentences pronounced by these haughty and wayward souls the rulers of the earth have wrought that which ye have heard. . . . The reins of the heedless masses have been, and are, in the hands of the exponents of idle fancies and vain imaginings. These decree what they please. God, verily, is clear of them, and We, too, are clear of them, as are such as have testified unto that which the Pen of the Most High hath spoken in this glorious Station.*"

"*The leaders of men,*" He has likewise asserted, "*have,* 198 *from time immemorial, prevented the people from turning unto the Most Great Ocean. The Friend of God* [Abraham] *was cast into fire through the sentence pronounced by the divines of the age, and lies and calumnies were imputed to Him Who discoursed with God* [Moses].

Reflect upon the One Who was the Spirit of God [Jesus]. *Though He showed forth the utmost compassion and tenderness, yet they rose up against that Essence of Being and Lord of the seen and unseen, in such a manner that He could find no refuge wherein to rest. Each day He wandered unto a new place, and sought a new shelter. Consider the Seal of the Prophets* [Muḥammad] *—may the souls of all else except Him be His sacrifice! How grievous the things which befell that Lord of all being at the hands of the priests of idolatry, and of the Jewish doctors, after He had uttered the blessed words proclaiming the unity of God! By My life! My pen groaneth, and all created things cry out by reason of the things that have touched Him, at the hands of such as have broken the Covenant of God and His Testament, and denied His Testimony, and gainsaid His signs."*

199   *"The foolish divines,"* another Tablet declares, *"have laid aside the Book of God, and are occupied with that which they themselves have fashioned. The Ocean of Knowledge is revealed, and the shrill of the Pen of the Most High is raised, and yet they, even as earthworms, are afflicted with the clay of their fancies and imaginings. They are exalted by reason of their relationship to the one true God, and yet they have turned aside from Him! Because of Him have they become famous, and yet they are shut off as by a veil from Him!"*

200   *"The pagan priests,"* in yet another Tablet is written, *"and the Jewish and Christian divines, have committed the very things which the divines of the age, in this Dispensation, have committed, and are still committing.*

*Nay, these have displayed a more grievous cruelty and a
fiercer malice. Every atom beareth witness unto that which
I say.*"

To these leaders who "*esteem themselves the best of* 201
*all creatures and have been regarded as the vilest by Him
Who is the Truth*," who "*occupy the seats of knowledge
and learning, and who have named ignorance knowledge, and called oppression justice*," and who, "*worship no
God but their own desire, who bear allegiance to naught
but gold, who are wrapt in the densest veils of learning,
and who, enmeshed by its obscurities, are lost in the wilds
of error*"—to these Bahá'u'lláh has chosen to address
these words: "*O concourse of divines! Ye shall not
henceforward behold yourselves possessed of any power,
inasmuch as We have seized it from you, and destined it
for such as have believed in God, the One, the All-Powerful, the Almighty, the Unconstrained.*"

In the Kitáb-i-Aqdas we read the following: "*Say:* 202
*O leaders of religion! Weigh not the Book of God with
such standards and sciences as are current amongst you,
for the Book itself is the unerring Balance established
amongst men. In this most perfect Balance whatsoever
the peoples and kindreds of the earth possess must be
weighed, while the measure of its weight should be tested
according to its own standard, did ye but know it. The
eye of My loving-kindness weepeth sore over you, inasmuch as ye have failed to recognize the One upon Whom
ye have been calling in the daytime and in the night season, at even and at morn. . . . O ye leaders of religion!
Who is the man amongst you that can rival Me in vision*

or insight? Where is he to be found that dareth to claim to be My equal in utterance or wisdom? No, by My Lord, the All-Merciful! All on the earth shall pass away; and this is the face of your Lord, the Almighty, the Well-Beloved. . . . Say: This, verily, is the heaven in which the Mother Book is treasured, could ye but comprehend it. He it is Who hath caused the Rock to shout, and the Burning Bush to lift up its voice, upon the Mount rising above the Holy Land, and proclaim: 'The Kingdom is God's, the sovereign Lord of all, the All-Powerful, the Loving!' We have not entered any school, nor read any of your dissertations. Incline your ears to the words of this unlettered One, wherewith He summoneth you unto God, the Ever-Abiding. Better is this for you than all the treasures of the earth, could ye but comprehend it."

203   *"O concourse of divines!"* He moreover has written, *"When My verses were sent down, and My clear tokens were revealed, We found you behind the veils. This, verily, is a strange thing. . . . We have rent the veils asunder. Beware lest ye shut out the people by yet another veil. Pluck asunder the chains of vain imaginings, in the name of the Lord of all men, and be not of the deceitful. Should ye turn unto God, and embrace His Cause, spread not disorder within it, and measure not the Book of God with your selfish desires. This, verily, is the counsel of God aforetime and hereafter. . . . Had ye believed in God, when He revealed Himself, the people would not have turned aside from Him, nor would the things ye witness today have befallen Us. Fear God, and be not of the heed-*

*less. . . . This is the Cause that hath caused all your su-
perstitions and idols to tremble. . . . O concourse of divines! Beware lest ye be the cause of strife in the land,
even as ye were the cause of the repudiation of the Faith in
its early days. Gather the people around this Word that
hath made the pebbles to cry out: 'The Kingdom is God's,
the Dawning-Place of all signs!' . . . Tear the veils asunder in such wise that the inmates of the Kingdom will
hear them being rent. This is the command of God, in
days gone by, and for those to come. Blessed the man that
observeth that whereunto he was bidden, and woe betide
the negligent."*

And again: *"How long will ye, O concourse of di-* 204
*vines, level the spears of hatred at the face of Bahá? Rein
in your pens. Lo, the Most Sublime Pen speaketh betwixt
earth and heaven. Fear God, and follow not your desires
which have altered the face of creation. Purify your ears
that they may hearken unto the Voice of God. By God! It
is even as fire that consumeth the veils, and as water that
washeth the souls of all who are in the universe."*

"Say: O concourse of divines!" He furthermore ad- 205
dresses them, *"Can any one of you race with the Divine
Youth in the arena of wisdom and utterance, or soar with
Him into the heaven of inner meaning and explanation?
Nay, by My Lord, the God of mercy! All have swooned
away in this Day from the Word of thy Lord. They are
even as dead and lifeless, except him whom thy Lord, the
Almighty, the Unconstrained, hath willed to exempt. Such
a one is indeed of those endued with knowledge in the*

sight of Him Who is the All-Knowing. The inmates of Paradise, and the dwellers of the sacred Folds, bless him at eventide and at dawn. Can the one possessed of wooden legs resist him whose feet God hath made of steel? Nay, by Him Who illumineth the whole of creation!"

206 "When We observed carefully," He significantly remarks, *"We discovered that Our enemies are, for the most part, the divines." "Among the people are those who said: 'He hath repudiated the divines.' Say: 'Yea, by My Lord! I, in very truth, was the One Who abolished the idols!'" "We, verily, have sounded the Trumpet, which is Our Most Sublime Pen, and lo, the divines and the learned, and the doctors and the rulers, swooned away except such as God preserved, as a token of His grace, and He, verily, is the All-Bounteous, the Ancient of Days."*

207 "O concourse of divines! Fling away idle fancies and imaginings, and turn, then, towards the Horizon of Certitude. I swear by God! All that ye possess will profit you not, neither all the treasures of the earth, nor the leadership ye have usurped. Fear God, and be not of the lost ones." "Say: O concourse of divines! Lay aside all your veils and coverings. Give ear unto that whereunto calleth you the Most Sublime Pen, in this wondrous Day. . . . The world is laden with dust, by reason of your vain imaginings, and the hearts of such as enjoy near access to God are troubled because of your cruelty. Fear God, and be of them that judge equitably."*

208 "O ye the dawning-places of knowledge!" He thus exhorts them, *"Beware that ye suffer not yourselves to be-*

*come changed, for as ye change, most men will, likewise,
change. This, verily, is an injustice unto yourselves and
unto others. . . . Ye are even as a spring. If it be changed,
so will the streams that branch out from it be changed.
Fear God, and be numbered with the godly. In like manner, if the heart of man be corrupted, his limbs will also
be corrupted. And similarly, if the root of a tree be corrupted, its branches, and its offshoots, and its leaves, and
its fruits, will be corrupted."*

    "Say: O concourse of divines!" He thus appeals to   209
them, *"Be fair, I adjure you by God, and nullify not the
Truth with the things ye possess. Peruse that which We
have sent down with truth. It will, verily, aid you, and
will draw you nigh unto God, the Mighty, the Great.
Consider and call to mind how when Muḥammad, the
Apostle of God, appeared, the people denied Him. They
ascribed unto Him what caused the Spirit [Jesus] to lament in His Most Sublime Station, and the Faithful
Spirit to cry out. Consider, moreover, the things which
befell the Apostles and Messengers of God before Him, by
reason of what the hands of the unjust have wrought. We
make mention of you for the sake of God, and remind you
of His signs, and announce unto you the things ordained
for such as are nigh unto Him in the most sublime Paradise and the all-highest Heaven, and I, verily, am the
Announcer, the Omniscient. He hath come for your salvation, and hath borne tribulations that ye may ascend, by
the ladder of utterance, unto the summit of understanding. . . . Peruse, with fairness and justice, that which*

hath been sent down. It will, verily, exalt you through the truth, and will cause you to behold the things from which ye have been withheld, and will enable you to quaff His sparkling Wine."

Words Addressed to Muslim Ecclesiastics

210 Let us now consider more particularly the specific references, and the words directly addressed, to Muslim ecclesiastics by the Báb and Bahá'u'lláh. The Báb, as attested by the Kitáb-i-Íqán, has *"specifically revealed an Epistle unto the divines of every city, wherein He hath fully set forth the character of the denial and repudiation of each of them."* Whilst in Iṣfahán, that time-honored stronghold of Muslim ecclesiasticism, He, through the medium of its governor, Manúchihr Khán, invited in writing the divines of that city to engage in a contest with Him, in order, as He expressed it, to *"establish the truth and dissipate falsehood."* Not one of the multitude of divines who thronged that great seat of learning had the courage to take up that challenge. Bahá'u'lláh, on His part, while in Adrianople, and as witnessed by His own Tablet to the Sháh of Persia, signified His wish to be *"brought face to face with the divines of the age, and produce proofs and testimonies in the presence of His Majesty, the Sháh."* This offer was denounced as a "great presumption and amazing audacity" by the divines of Ṭihrán, who, in their fear, advised their sovereign to instantly punish the bearer of that Tablet.

Previously, while Bahá'u'lláh was in Baghdád, He expressed His willingness that, provided the divines of Najaf and Karbilá—the twin holiest cities next to Mecca and Medina, in the eyes of the Shí'ihs—assembled and agreed regarding any miracle they wished to be performed, and signed and sealed a statement affirming that on performance of this miracle they would acknowledge the truth of His Mission, He would unhesitatingly produce it. To this challenge they, as recorded by 'Abdu'l-Bahá in His "Some Answered Questions," could offer no better reply than this: "This man is an enchanter; perhaps he will perform an enchantment, and then we shall have nothing more to say." *"For twelve years,"* Bahá'u'lláh Himself has testified, *"We tarried in Baghdád. Much as We desired that a large gathering of divines and fair-minded men be convened, so that truth might be distinguished from falsehood, and be fully demonstrated, no action was taken."* And again: *"And likewise, while in 'Iráq, We wished to come together with the divines of Persia. No sooner did they hear of this, than they fled and said: 'He indeed is a manifest sorcerer!' This is the word that proceeded aforetime out of the mouths of such as were like them. These* [divines] *objected to what they said, and yet, they themselves repeat, in this day, what was said before them, and understand not. By My life! They are even as ashes in the sight of thy Lord. If He be willing, tempestuous gales will blow over them, and make them as dust. Thy Lord, verily, doth what He pleaseth."*

These false, these cruel and cowardly Shí'ih cleri- 211

cals, who, as Bahá'u'lláh declared, had they not intervened, Persia would have been subdued by the power
of God in hardly more than two years, have been thus
addressed in the Qayyúm-i-Asmá': *"O concourse of divines! Fear God from this day onwards in the views ye
advance, for He Who is Our Remembrance in your midst,
and Who cometh from Us, is, in very truth, the Judge and
Witness. Turn away from that which ye lay hold of, and
which the Book of God, the True One, hath not sanc-
tioned, for on the Day of Resurrection ye shall, upon the
Bridge, be, in very truth, held answerable for the position
ye occupied."*

212   In that same Book the Báb thus addresses the
<u>Shí</u>'ihs, as well as the entire body of the followers of
the Prophet: *"O concourse of <u>Shí</u>'ihs! Fear ye God, and
Our Cause, which concerneth Him Who is the Most Great
Remembrance of God. For great is its fire, as decreed in
the Mother-Book." "O people of the Qur'án! Ye are as nothing unless ye submit unto the Remembrance of God and
unto this Book. If ye follow the Cause of God, We will
forgive you your sins, and if ye turn aside from Our command, We will, in truth, condemn your souls in Our Book,
unto the Most Great Fire. We, verily, do not deal unjustly
with men, even to the extent of a speck on a date stone."*

213   And finally, in that same Commentary, this startling prophecy is recorded: *"Erelong We will, in very
truth, torment such as waged war against Ḥusayn* [Imám
Ḥusayn], *in the Land of the Euphrates, with the most
afflictive torment, and the most dire and exemplary pun-*

ishment." "*Erelong,*" He also, referring to that same people, in that same Book, has written, "*will God wreak His vengeance upon them, at the time of Our Return, and He hath, in very truth, prepared for them, in the world to come, a severe torment.*"

As to Bahá'u'lláh, the passages I cite in these pages 214 constitute but a fraction of the references to the Muslim divines with which His writings abound. "*The Lote-Tree beyond Which there is no passing,*" He exclaims, "*crieth out, by reason of the cruelty of the divines. It shouteth aloud, and bewaileth itself.*" "*From the inception of this sect* [Shí'ih]," He, in His "Epistle to the Son of the Wolf," has written, "*until the present day, how great hath been the number of the divines that have appeared, none of whom became cognizant of the nature of this Revelation. What could have been the cause of this waywardness? Were We to mention it, their limbs would cleave asunder. It is necessary for them to meditate, nay to meditate for a thousand thousand years, that haply they may attain unto a sprinkling from the ocean of knowledge, and discover the things whereof they are oblivious in this day. I was walking in the Land of Ṭá* [Ṭihrán] —*the dayspring of the signs of thy Lord—when lo, I heard the lamentation of the pulpits and the voice of their supplication unto God, blessed and glorified be He! They cried out and said: 'O God of the world and Lord of the nations! Thou beholdest our state and the things which have befallen us, by reason of the cruelty of Thy servants. Thou hast created us and revealed us for Thy glorification and praise. Thou dost now hear what the wayward proclaim upon us in Thy days. By Thy might! Our souls are melted, and our limbs are trembling. Alas, alas! Would that we had never been created and revealed by Thee!' The hearts of them that enjoy near access to God are consumed by these words, and from them the cries of such as are devoted to Him are raised."*

215   "*These thick clouds,*" He, in that same Epistle, has stated, "*are the exponents of idle fancies and vain imaginings, who are none other than the divines of Persia.*" "*By 'divines' in the passage cited above,*" He, in that same connection, explains, "*is meant those men who outwardly attire themselves with the raiment of knowledge, but who inwardly are deprived therefrom. In this connection We quote, from the Tablet addressed to His Majesty the Sháh, certain passages from the 'Hidden Words' which were revealed by the Abhá Pen under the name of the 'Book of Fáṭimih,' the blessings of God be upon her!' 'O ye that are foolish, yet have a name to be wise! Wherefore do ye wear the guise of the shepherd, when inwardly ye have become wolves, intent upon My flock? Ye are even as the star, which riseth ere the dawn, and which, though it seem radiant and luminous, leadeth the wayfarers of My city astray into the paths of perdition.' And likewise He saith: 'O ye seemingly fair yet inwardly foul! Ye are like clear but bitter water, which to outward seeming is but crystal pure but of which, when tested by the Divine Assayer, not a drop is accepted. Yea, the sunbeam falleth alike upon the dust and the mirror, yet differ they in reflection even*

as doth the star from the earth: nay, immeasurable is the difference!'"

"*We have invited all men,*" Bahá'u'lláh, in another 216
Tablet, has stated, "*to turn towards God, and have acquainted them with the Straight Path. They* [divines] *rose up against Us with such cruelty as hath sapped the strength of Islám, and yet most of the people are heedless!*" "*The children of Him Who is the Friend of God* [Abraham]," He moreover has written, "*and heirs of the One Who discoursed with God* [Moses], *who were accounted the most abject of men, have split the veils asunder, and rent the coverings, and seized the Sealed Wine from the hands of the bounty of Him Who is the Self-Subsisting, and drunk their fill, whilst the detestable Shí'ih divines have remained, until the present time, hesitant and perverse.*" And again: "*The divines of Persia committed that which no people amongst the peoples of the world have committed.*"

"*If this Cause be of God,*" He thus addresses the 217
Minister of the Sháh in Constantinople, "*no man can prevail against it; and if it be not of God, the divines amongst you, and they that follow their corrupt desires, and such as have rebelled against Him, will surely suffice to overpower it.*"

"*Of all the peoples of the world,*" He, in another 218
Tablet, observes, "*they that have suffered the greatest loss have been, and are still, the people of Persia. I swear by the Daystar of Utterance which shineth upon the world in its meridian glory! The lamentations of the pulpits, in*

that country, are being raised continually. In the early days such lamentations were heard in the Land of Ṭá [Ṭihrán], for pulpits, erected for the purpose of remembering the True One—exalted be His glory—have now, in Persia, become places wherefrom blasphemies are uttered against Him Who is the Desire of the worlds."

219   "In this day," is His caustic denunciation, "the world is redolent with the fragrances of the robe of the Revelation of the Ancient King . . . and yet, they [divines] have gathered together, and established themselves upon their seats, and have spoken that which would put an animal to shame, how much more man himself! Were they to become aware of one of their acts, and perceive the mischief it hath wrought, they would, with their own hands, dispatch themselves to their final abode."

220   "O concourse of divines!" Bahá'u'lláh thus commands them, ". . . Lay aside that which ye possess, and hold your peace, and give ear, then, unto that which the Tongue of Grandeur and Majesty speaketh. How many the veiled handmaidens who turned unto Me, and believed, and how numerous the wearers of the turban who were debarred from Me, and followed in the footsteps of bygone generations!"

221   "I swear by the Daystar that shineth above the Horizon of Utterance!" He asserts, "A paring from the nail of one of the believing handmaidens is, in this day, more esteemed, in the sight of God, than the divines of Persia, who, after thirteen hundred years' waiting, have perpetrated what the Jews have not perpetrated during the Revelation of Him Who is the Spirit [Jesus]." "Though they

rejoice," is His warning, *"at the adversities that have touched Us, the day will come whereon they shall wail and weep."*

"O heedless one!" He thus addresses, in the Lawḥ-i-Burhán, a notorious Persian mujtahid, whose hands were stained with the blood of Bahá'í martyrs, *"rely not on thy glory and thy power. Thou art even as the last trace of sunlight upon the mountaintop. Soon will it fade away, as decreed by God, the All-Possessing, the Most High. Thy glory, and the glory of such as are like thee, have been taken away, and this, verily, is what hath been ordained by the One with Whom is the Mother Tablet. . . . Because of you the Apostle [Muḥammad] lamented, and the Chaste One [Fáṭimih] cried out, and the countries were laid waste, and darkness fell upon all regions. O concourse of divines! Because of you the people were abased, and the banner of Islám was hauled down, and its mighty throne subverted. Every time a man of discernment hath sought to hold fast unto that which would exalt Islám, you raised a clamor, and thereby was he deterred from achieving his purpose, while the land remained fallen in clear ruin."* 222

"Say: O concourse of Persian divines!" Bahá'u'lláh again prophesies, *"In My name ye have seized the reins of men, and occupy the seats of honor, by reason of your relation to Me. When I revealed Myself, however, ye turned aside, and committed what hath caused the tears of such as have recognized Me to flow. Erelong will all that ye possess perish, and your glory be turned into the most wretched abasement, and ye shall behold the punishment* 223

for what ye have wrought, as decreed by God, the Ordainer, the All-Wise."

224   In the Súriy-i-Mulúk, addressing the entire company of the ecclesiastical leaders of Sunní Islám in Constantinople, the capital of the Empire and seat of the Caliphate, He has written: *"O ye divines of the City! We came to you with the truth, whilst ye were heedless of it. Methinks ye are as dead, wrapt in the coverings of your own selves. Ye sought not Our presence, when so to do would have been better for you than all your doings. . . . Know ye, that had your leaders, to whom ye owe allegiance, and on whom ye pride yourselves, and whom ye mention by day and by night, and from whose traces ye seek guidance—had they lived in these days, they would have circled around Me, and would not have separated themselves from Me, whether at eventide or at morn. Ye, however, did not turn your faces towards My face, for even less than a moment, and waxed proud, and were careless of this Wronged One, Who hath been so afflicted by men that they dealt with Him as they pleased. Ye failed to inquire about My condition, nor did ye inform yourselves of the things which befell Me. Thereby have ye withheld from yourselves the winds of holiness, and the breezes of bounty, that blow from this luminous and perspicuous Spot. Methinks ye have clung to outward things, and forgotten the inner things, and say that which ye do not. Ye are lovers of names, and appear to have given yourselves up to them. For this reason make ye mention of the names of your leaders. And should anyone like them, or superior unto them, come unto you, ye would flee him. Through*

*their names ye have exalted yourselves, and have secured
your positions, and live and prosper. And were your leaders to reappear, ye would not renounce your leadership,
nor would ye turn in their direction, nor set your faces
towards them. We found you, as We found most men,
worshiping names which they mention during the days of
their life, and with which they occupy themselves. No sooner
do the Bearers of these names appear, however, than they
repudiate them, and turn upon their heels. . . . Know ye
that God will not, in this day, accept your thoughts, nor
your remembrance of Him, nor your turning towards
Him, nor your devotions, nor your vigilance, unless ye be
made new in the estimation of this Servant, could ye but
perceive it."*

The voice of 'Abdu'l-Bahá, the Center of the Cov-   225
enant of God, has, likewise, been raised, announcing
the dire misfortunes which were to overtake, soon after His passing, the ecclesiastical hierarchies of both
Sunní and Shí'ih Islám. *"This glory,"* He has written,
*"shall be turned into the most abject abasement, and this
pomp and might converted into the most complete subju-
gation. Their palaces will be transformed into prisons,
and the course of their ascendant star terminate in the
depths of the pit. Laughter and merriment will vanish,
nay more, the voice of their weeping will be raised." "Even
as the snow,"* He moreover has written, *"they will melt
away in the July sun."*

The dissolution of the institution of the Caliph-   226
ate, the complete secularization of the state which had
enshrined the most august institution of Islám, and

the virtual collapse of the Shí'ih hierarchy in Persia, were the visible and immediate consequences of the treatment meted out to the Cause of God by the clergy of the two largest communions of the Muslim world.

The Falling Fortunes of Shí'ih Islám

227 Let us first consider the visitations that have marked the falling fortunes of Shí'ih Islám. The iniquities summarized in the beginning of these pages, and for which the Shí'ih ecclesiastical order in Persia is to be held primarily answerable; iniquities which, in the words of Bahá'u'lláh, had caused *"the Apostle* [Muḥammad] *to lament, and the Chaste One* [Fáṭimih] *to cry out,"* and *"all created things to groan, and the limbs of the holy ones to quake"*; iniquities which had riddled the breast of the Báb with bullets, and bowed down Bahá'u'lláh, and turned His hair white, and caused Him to groan aloud in anguish, and made Muḥammad to weep over Him, and Jesus to beat Himself upon the head, and the Báb to bewail His plight—such iniquities indeed could not, and were not to, remain unpunished. God, the fiercest of Avengers, was lying in wait, pledged *"not to forgive any man's injustice."* The scourge of His chastisement, swift, sudden and terrible, was, at long last, let loose upon the perpetrators of these iniquities.

228 A revolution, formidable in its proportions, far-reaching in its repercussions, amazing in the absence

of bloodshed and even of violence which marked its progress, challenged that ecclesiastical ascendancy which, for centuries, had been of the essence of Islám in that country, and virtually overthrew a hierarchy with which the machinery of the state and the life of the people had been inextricably interwoven. Such a revolution did not signalize the disestablishment of a state-church. It indeed was tantamount to the disruption of what may be called a church-state—a state that had been hopefully awaiting, even up till the moment of its expiry, the gladsome advent of the Hidden Imám, who would not only seize the reins of authority from the sháh, the chief magistrate who was merely representing him, but would also assume dominion over the whole earth.

The spirit which that clerical order had so assidu- 229
ously striven, during a whole century, to crush; the Faith which it had, with such ferocious brutality, attempted to extirpate; were now, in their turn, through the forces they had engendered in the world, deranging the equilibrium, and sapping the strength, of that same order whose ramifications had extended to every sphere, duty, and act of life in that country. The rock wall of Islám, seemingly impregnable, was now shaken to its foundations, and was tottering to its ruin, before the very eyes of the persecuted followers of the Faith of Bahá'u'lláh. A sacerdotal hierarchy that had held in thrall for so long the Faith of God, and seemed, at one time, to have mortally struck it down, now found itself the prey of a superior civil authority whose settled

policy was to fasten, steadily and relentlessly, its coils around it.

230   The vast system of that hierarchy, with all its elements and appurtenances—its sha_ykhu'l-Isláms (high priests), its mujtahids (doctors of the law), its mullás (priests), its fuqahá's (jurists), its imáms (prayer-leaders), its mu'adhdhins (criers), its vu'ázz (preachers), its qáḍís (judges), its mutavallís (custodians), its madrasihs (seminaries), its mudarrisíns (professors), its ṭullábs (pupils), its qurrá's (intoners), its mu'abbiríns (soothsayers), its muhaddithíns (narrators), its musakhkhiríns (spirit-subduers), its dhákiríns (rememberers), its 'ummál-i-dhakát (almsgivers), its muqaddasíns (saints), its munzavís (recluses), its ṣúfís, its dervishes, and what not—was paralyzed and utterly discredited. Its mujtahids, those firebrands, who wielded powers of life and death, and who for generations had been accorded honors almost regal in character, were reduced to a deplorably insignificant number. The beturbaned prelates of the Islamic church who, in the words of Bahá'u'lláh, *"decked their heads with green and white, and committed what made the Faithful Spirit to groan"* were ruthlessly swept away, except for a handful who, in order to safeguard themselves against the fury of an impious populace, are now compelled to submit to the humiliation of producing, whenever the occasion demands it, the license granted them by the civil authorities to wear this vanishing emblem of a vanished authority. The rest of this turbaned class, whether

siyyids, mullás, or hájís, were forced not only to exchange their venerable headdress for the kuláh-i-farangí (European hat), which not long ago they themselves had anathematized, but also to discard their flowing robes and don the tight-fitting garments of European style, the introduction of which into their country they had, a generation ago, so violently disapproved.

"The dark blue and white domes"—an allusion by 231 'Abdu'l-Bahá to the rotund and massive headgears of the priests of Persia—had indeed been *"inverted."* Those whose heads had borne them, the arrogant, fanatical, perfidious, and retrograde clericals, *"in the grasp of whose authority,"* as testified by Bahá'u'lláh, *"were held the reins of the people,"* whose *"words are the pride of the world,"* and whose *"deeds are the shame of the nations,"* recognizing the wretchedness of their state, betook themselves, crestfallen and destitute of hope, to their homes, there to drag out a miserable existence. Impotent and sullen, they are watching the operations of a process which, having reversed their policy and ruined their handiwork, is irresistibly moving towards a climax.

The pomp and pageantry of these princes of the 232 church of Islám has already died out. Their fanatical outcries, their clamorous invocations, their noisy demonstrations, are stilled. Their fatvás (sentences), pronounced with such shamelessness, and at times embracing the denunciation of kings, are a dead letter. The spectacular sight of congregational prayers, in which thousands of worshipers, lined row upon row, participated, has vanished. The pulpits from whence they discharged the thunder of their anathemas against the powerful and the innocent alike, are deserted and silent. Their waqfs, those priceless and far-flung endowments—the landed property of the expected Imám—which in Iṣfahán alone at one time embraced the whole of the city, have been wrested out of their hands, and brought under the control of a lay administration. Their madrasihs (seminaries), with their medieval learning, are deserted and dilapidated. The innumerable tomes of theological commentaries, super-commentaries, glosses, and notes, unreadable, unprofitable, the product of misdirected ingenuity and toil, and pronounced by one of the most enlightened Islamic thinkers in modern times as works obscuring sound knowledge, breeding maggots, and fit for fire, are now buried away, overspread with cobwebs, and forgotten. Their abstruse dissertations, their vehement controversies, their interminable discussions, are outmoded and abandoned. Their masjids (mosques) and imám-zádihs (tombs of saints), which were privileged to extend the bast (right of sanctuary) to many a criminal, and which had degenerated into a monstrous scandal, whose walls rang with the intonations of a hypocritical and profligate clergy, whose ornaments vied with the treasures of the palaces of kings, are either forsaken or fallen in ruin. Their takyihs, the haunts of the lazy, the passive, and contemplative pietists, are either being sold or closed down. Their taʻzíyihs (religious plays), acted with barbaric zeal, and accentuated by sudden spasms of unbridled religious excitement, are forbidden. Even their rawḍih-khánís (lamentations), with their long-drawn-out, plaintive howls, which arose from so many houses, have been curtailed and discouraged. The sacred pilgrimages to Najaf and Karbilá, the holiest shrines of the Shí'ih world, are reduced in number and made increasingly difficult, preventing thereby many a greedy mullá from indulging in his time-honored habit of charging double for making those pilgrimages as a substitute for the religious-minded. The disuse of the veil which the mullás fought tooth and nail to prevent; the equality of sexes which their law forbade; the erection of civil tribunals which superseded their ecclesiastical courts; the abolition of the síghih (concubinage) which, when contracted for short periods, is hardly distinguishable from quasi-prostitution, and which made of the turbulent and fanatical Mashhad, the national center of pilgrimage, one of the most immoral cities in Asia; and finally, the efforts which are being made to disparage the Arabic tongue, the sacred language of Islám and of the Qur'án, and to divorce it from Persian—all these have successively lent their share to the acceleration of that impelling process which has subordinated to the civil authority the position and interests of Muslim clericals to a degree undreamt of by any mullá.

Well might the once lofty-turbaned, long-bearded, 233 grave-looking áqá (mullá), who had so insolently concerned himself with every department of human activity, as he sits, hatless, clean shaven, in the seclusion of his home, and perhaps listening to the strains of western music, blared upon the ethers of his native land, pause to reflect for a while on the vanished splendors of his defunct empire. Well might he muse upon the havoc which the rising tide of nationalism and skepticism has wrought in the adamantine traditions of his country. Well might he recollect the halcyon days when, seated on a donkey, and parading through the bázárs and maydáns of his native town, an eager but deluded multitude would rush to kiss with fervor not only his hands, but also the tail of the animal on which he rode. Well might he remember the blind zeal with which they acclaimed his acts, and the prodigies and miracles they ascribed to their performance.

234   He might indeed look back further, and call to mind the reign of those pious Ṣafaví monarchs, who delighted to call themselves "dogs of the threshold of the Immaculate Imáms," how one of those kings was induced to go on foot before the mujtahid as he rode through the maydán-i-Sháh, the main square of Iṣfahán, as a mark of royal subservience to the favorite minister of the Hidden Imám, a minister who, as distinct from the Sháh's title, styled himself "the servant of the Lord of Saintship (Imám 'Alí)."

235   Was it not, he might well ponder, this same Sháh 'Abbás the Great who had been arrogantly addressed by another mujtahid as "the founder of a borrowed empire," implying that the kingdom of the "king of kings" really belonged to the expected Imám, and was

held by the Sháh solely in the capacity of a temporary
trustee? Was it not this same Sháh who walked the
entire distance of eight hundred miles from Iṣfahán to
Mashhad, the "special glory of the Shí'ih world," to
offer his prayers, in the only way that befitted the
sháhansháh, at the shrine of the Imám Riḍá, and who
trimmed the thousand candles which adorned its
courts? Had not Sháh Ṭahmasp, on receiving an epistle,
penned by yet another mujtahid, sprung to his feet,
placed it on his eyes, kissed it with rapture, and, because he had been addressed as "brother," ordered it
to be placed within his winding-sheet and buried with
him?

Might not that same mullá ponder the torrents of 236
blood which, during the long years when he enjoyed
impunity of conduct, flowed at his behest, the flam-
boyant anathemas he pronounced, and the great army
of orphans and widows, of the disinherited, the dis-
honored, the destitute, and the homeless which, on
the Day of Reckoning, were, with one accord, to cry
out for vengeance, and invoke the malediction of God
upon him?

That infamous crew had indeed merited the deg- 237
radation in which it had sunk. Persistently ignoring
the sentence of doom which the finger of Bahá'u'lláh
had traced upon the wall, it pursued, for well nigh a
hundred years, its fatal course, until, at the appointed
hour, its death knell was sounded by those spiritual,
revolutionary forces which, synchronizing with the first

dawnings of the World Order of His Faith, are upsetting the equilibrium, and throwing into such confusion, the ancient institutions of mankind.

The Collapse of the Caliphate

238   These same forces, operating in a collateral field, have effected a still more remarkable, and a more radical, revolution, culminating in the collapse and fall of the Muslim Caliphate, the most powerful institution of the whole Islamic world. This event of portentous significance has, moreover, been followed by a formal and definite separation of what was left of the Sunní faith in Turkey from the state, and by the complete secularization of the Republic that has arisen on the ruins of the Ottoman theocratic empire. This catastrophic fall, that stunned the Islamic world, and the avowed, the unqualified, and formal divorce between the spiritual and temporal powers, which distinguished the revolution in Turkey from that which occurred in Persia, I now proceed to consider.

239   Sunní Islám has sustained, not through the action of a foreign and invading Power, but at the hands of a dictator, avowedly professing the Faith of Muḥammad, a blow more grievous than that which fell, almost simultaneously, upon its sister-sect in Persia. This retributive act, directed against the archenemy of the Faith of Bahá'u'lláh, recalls a similar disaster precipitated through the action of a Roman emperor, during

the latter part of the first century of the Christian era—
a disaster that razed to its foundations the Temple of
Solomon, destroyed the Holy of Holies, laid waste the
city of David, uprooted the Jewish hierarchy in Jerusalem, massacred thousands of the Jewish people—the
persecutors of the religion of Jesus Christ—dispersed
the remainder over the surface of the earth, and reared
a pagan colony on Zion.

The Caliph, the self-styled vicar of the Prophet of 240
Islám, exercised a spiritual sovereignty, and was invested with a sacred character, which the Sháh of Persia neither claimed nor possessed. Nor should it be
forgotten that the sphere of his spiritual jurisdiction
extended to countries far beyond the confines of his
own empire, and embraced the overwhelming majority of Muslims throughout the world. He was, moreover, in his capacity as the Prophet's representative on
earth, regarded as the protector of the holy cities of
Mecca and Medina, the defender and propagator of
Islám, and the commander of its followers in any holy
war they might be called upon to wage.

So potent, so august, so sacred a personage was at 241
first by virtue of the abolition of the Sultanate in Turkey, divested of that temporal authority which the exponents of the Sunní school have regarded as a necessary concomitant to his high office. The sword, emblem of temporal sovereignty, was thus wrested out of
the hands of the commander who, for a brief period,
was permitted to occupy such an anomalous and pre-
carious position. It was soon, however, trumpeted to

the Sunní world, which had not previously been in the least consulted, that the Caliphate itself had been extinguished, and that the country which had accepted it as an appanage to its Sultanate, for more than four hundred years, had now permanently disowned it. The Turks who had been the militant leaders of the Muḥammadan world, since the Arab decline, and who had carried the standard of Islám as far as the gates of Vienna, the seat of government of Europe's premier Power, had resigned their leadership. The ex-caliph, shorn of his royal pomp, stripped of the symbols of his vicarship, and deserted by friend and foe alike, was forced to flee from Constantinople, the proud seat of a dual sovereignty, to the land of the infidels, resigning himself to that same life of exile to which a number of his fellow-sovereigns had been and were still condemned.

242   Nor has the Sunní world, despite determined efforts, succeeded in designating anyone in his stead who, though deprived of the sword of a commander, would still act as the custodian of the cloak and standard of the Apostle of God—the twin holy symbols of the Caliphate. Conferences were held, discussions ensued, a Congress of the Caliphate was convened in the Egyptian capital, the City of the Fatimites, only to result in the widely advertised and public confession of its failure: "They have agreed to disagree!"

243   Strange, incredibly strange, must appear the position of this most powerful branch of the Islamic Faith, with no outward and visible head to voice its senti-

ments and convictions, its unity irretrievably shattered, its radiance obscured, its law undermined, its institutions thrown into hopeless confusion. This institution that had challenged the inalienable, divinely appointed rights of the Imáms of the Faith of Muḥammad, had, after the revolution of thirteen centuries, vanished like a smoke, an institution which had dealt such merciless blows to a Faith Whose Herald was Himself a descendant of the Imáms, the lawful successors of the Apostle of God.

To what else could this remarkable prophecy, enshrined in the Lawḥ-i-Burhán, allude if not to the downfall of this crowned overlord of Sunní Muslims? *"O concourse of Muslim Divines! Because of you the people were abased, and the banner of Islám was hauled down, and its mighty throne subverted."* What of the indubitably clear and amazing prophecy recorded in the Qayyúm-i-Asmá'? *"Erelong We will, in very truth, torment such as waged war against Ḥusayn* [Imám Ḥusayn], *in the Land of the Euphrates, with the most afflictive torment, and the direst and most exemplary punishment."* What other interpretation can this Muḥammadan tradition be given? *"In the latter days a grievous calamity shall befall My people at the hands of their ruler, a calamity such as no man ever heard to surpass it."*

This was not all, however. The disappearance of the Caliph, the spiritual head of above two hundred million Muḥammadans, brought in its wake, in the land that had dealt Islám such a heavy blow, the annulment of the sharí'ah canonical Law, the disen-

244

245

dowment of Sunní institutions, the promulgation of a civil Code, the suppression of religious orders, the abrogation of ceremonials and traditions inculcated by the religion of Muḥammad. The Shaykhu'l-Islám and his satellites, including muftís, qáḍís, ḥujahs, shaykhs, ṣúfís, ḥájís, mawlavís, dervishes, and others, vanished at a stroke more determined, more open, and drastic than the one dealt the Shí'ihs by the Sháh and his government. The mosques of the capital, the pride and glory of the Islamic world, were deserted, and the fairest and most famous of them all, the peerless St. Sophia, "the Second Firmament," "the Vehicle of the Cherubim," converted by the blatant creators of a secular regime into a museum. The Arabic tongue, the language of the Prophet of God, was banished from the land, its alphabet was superseded by Latin characters, and the Qur'án itself translated into Turkish for the few who still cared to read it. The constitution of the new Turkey not only proclaimed formally the disestablishment and disendowment of Islám, with all its attendant and, in the view of some, atheistic enactments, but also heralded various measures that aimed at its further humiliation and weakening. Even the city of Constantinople, "the Dome of Islám," apostrophized in such condemnatory terms by Bahá'u'lláh, which, after the fall of Byzantium, had been hailed by the great Constantine as "the New Rome," and exalted to the rank of the metropolis of both the Roman Empire and of Christendom, and subsequently revered as the seat of the Caliphs, was relegated to the position of a provincial city and stripped of all its pomp and glory, its soaring and slender minarets standing sentinel at the grave of so much vanished splendor and power.

"O Spot that art situate on the shores of the two seas!" 246 Bahá'u'lláh has thus apostrophized the Imperial City, in terms that call to mind the prophetic words addressed by Jesus Christ to Jerusalem, *"The throne of tyranny hath, verily, been stablished upon thee, and the flame of hatred hath been kindled within thy bosom, in such wise that the Concourse on high, and they who circle around the Exalted Throne, have wailed and lamented. We behold in thee the foolish ruling over the wise, and darkness vaunting itself against the light. Thou art indeed filled with manifest pride. Hath thine outward splendor made thee vainglorious? By Him Who is the Lord of mankind! It shall soon perish, and thy daughters, and thy widows, and all the kindreds that dwell within thee shall lament. Thus informeth thee the All-Knowing, the All-Wise."*

Such was the fate that overtook both Shí'ih and 247 Sunní Islám, in the two countries where they had planted their banners and reared their most powerful and far-famed institutions. Such was their fate in these two countries, in one of which Bahá'u'lláh died an exile, and in the other the Báb suffered a martyr's death. Such was the fate of the self-styled Vicar of the Prophet of God, and of the favorite ministers of the still awaited Imám. *"The people of the Qur'án,"* Bahá'u'lláh testifies, *"have risen against Us, and tormented Us with such a torment that the Holy Spirit lamented, and the thunder roared out, and the clouds wept over Us. . . . Muḥammad, the Apostle of God, bewaileth, in the all-highest Paradise, their acts."* *"A day shall be witnessed by My people,"* their own traditions condemn them, *"whereon there will have remained of Islám naught but a name, and of the Qur'án naught but a mere appearance. The doctors of that age shall be the most evil the world hath ever seen. Mischief hath proceeded from them, and on them it will recoil."* And again: *"Most of His enemies will be the divines. His bidding they will not obey, but will protest saying: 'This is contrary to that which hath been handed down unto us by the Imáms of the Faith.'"* And still again: *"At that hour His malediction shall descend upon you, and your curse shall afflict you, and your religion shall remain an empty word on your tongues. And when these signs appear amongst you, anticipate the day when the red-hot wind will have swept over you, or the day when ye will have been disfigured, or when stones will have rained upon you."*

A Warning Unto All Nations

248   This horde of degraded priests, stigmatized by Bahá'u'lláh as *"doctors of doubt,"* as the *"abject manifestations of the Prince of Darkness,"* as *"wolves"* and *"pharaohs,"* as *"focal centers of hellish fire,"* as *"voracious beasts*

preying upon the carrion of the souls of men," and, as testified by their own traditions, as both the sources and victims of mischief, have joined the various swarms of s͟háh-zádihs, of emirs, and princelings of fallen dynasties—a witness and a warning unto all nations of what must, sooner or later, befall those wielders of earthly dominion, be it royal or ecclesiastic, who might dare to challenge or persecute the appointed Channels and Embodiments of Divine authority and power.

Islám, at once the progenitor and persecutor of 249 the Faith of Bahá'u'lláh, is, if we read aright the signs of the times, only beginning to sustain the impact of this invincible and triumphant Faith. We need only recall the nineteen hundred years of abject misery and dispersion which they, who only for the short space of three years persecuted the Son of God, have had to endure, and are still enduring. We may well ask ourselves, with mingled feelings of dread and awe, how severe must be the tribulations of those who, during no less than fifty years, have, *"at every moment tormented with a fresh torment"* Him Who is the Father, and who have, in addition, made His Herald—Himself a Manifestation of God—to quaff, in such tragic circumstances, the cup of martyrdom.

I have, in the pages immediately preceding, quoted 250 certain passages addressed collectively to the members of the ecclesiastical order, both Islamic and Christian, and have then recorded a number of specific addresses and references to Muslim divines, both S͟hí'ih and

Sunní, after which I proceeded to describe the calamities that afflicted these Muḥammadan hierarchies, their heads, their members, their properties, their ceremonials, and institutions. Let us now consider the addresses specifically made to the members of the Christian clerical order who, for the most part, have ignored the Faith of Bahá'u'lláh, whilst a few among them have, as its Administrative Order gained in stature and spread its ramifications over Christian countries, arisen to check its progress, to belittle its influence, and obscure its purpose.

His Messages to Christian Leaders

251 A glance at the writings of the Author of the Bahá'í Revelation will reveal the important and significant fact that He Who addressed collectively an immortal message to all the kings of the earth, Who revealed a Tablet to each of the outstanding crowned heads of Europe and Asia, Who issued His call to the sacerdotal leaders of Islám, both Sunní and Shí'ih, Who did not exclude from His purview the Jews and the Zoroastrians, has, apart from His numerous and repeated exhortations and warnings to the entire Christian world, directed particular messages, some general, others precise and challenging, to the heads, as well as to the rank and file, of the ecclesiastical orders of Christendom—its pope, its kings, its patriarchs, its

archbishops, its bishops, its priests, and its monks. We have already, in connection with the messages of Bahá'u'lláh to the crowned heads of the world, considered certain features of the Tablet to the Roman Pontiff, as well as the words written to the kings of Christendom. Let us now turn our attention to those passages in which the aristocracy of the church and its ordained servants are singled out for exhortation and admonition by the Pen of Bahá'u'lláh:

"Say: O concourse of patriarchs! He Whom ye were 252 promised in the Tablets is come. Fear God, and follow not the vain imaginings of the superstitious. Lay aside the things ye possess, and take fast hold of the Tablet of God by His sovereign power. Better is this for you than all your possessions. Unto this testifieth every understanding heart, and every man of insight. Pride ye yourselves on My Name, and yet shut yourselves out as by a veil from Me? This indeed is a strange thing!"

"Say: O concourse of archbishops! He Who is the Lord 253 of all men hath appeared. In the plain of guidance He calleth mankind, whilst ye are numbered with the dead! Great is the blessedness of him who is stirred by the Breeze of God, and hath arisen from amongst the dead in this perspicuous Name."

"Say: O concourse of bishops! Trembling hath seized 254 all the kindreds of the earth, and He Who is the Everlasting Father calleth aloud between earth and heaven. Blessed the ear that hath heard, and the eye that hath seen, and the heart that hath turned unto Him Who is the Point of

Adoration of all who are in the heavens and all who are on earth." "O concourse of bishops! Ye are the stars of the heaven of My knowledge. My mercy desireth not that ye should fall upon the earth. My justice, however, declareth: 'This is that which the Son [Jesus] *hath decreed.' And whatsoever hath proceeded out of His blameless, His truthspeaking, trustworthy mouth, can never be altered. The bells, verily, peal out My Name, and lament over Me, but My spirit rejoiceth with evident gladness. The body of the Loved One yearneth for the cross, and His head is eager for the spear, in the path of the All-Merciful. The ascendancy of the oppressor can in no wise deter Him from His purpose."* And again: *"The stars of the heaven of knowledge have fallen, they that adduce the proofs they possess in order to demonstrate the truth of My Cause, and who make mention of God in My Name. When I came unto them, in My majesty, however, they turned aside from Me. They, verily, are of the fallen. This is what the Spirit* [Jesus] *prophesied when He came with the truth, and the Jewish doctors caviled at Him, until they committed what made the Holy Spirit to lament, and the eyes of such as enjoy near access to God to weep."*

255 *"Say: O concourse of priests! Leave the bells, and come forth, then, from your churches. It behooveth you, in this day, to proclaim aloud the Most Great Name among the nations. Prefer ye to be silent, whilst every stone and every tree shouteth aloud: 'The Lord is come in His great glory!'? . . . He that summoneth men in My name is, verily, of Me, and he will show forth that which is beyond the power*

of all that are on earth. . . . Let the Breeze of God awaken you. Verily, it hath wafted over the world. Well is it with him that hath discovered the fragrance thereof and been accounted among the well-assured." And again: "O concourse of priests! The Day of Reckoning hath appeared, the Day whereon He Who was in heaven hath come. He, verily, is the One Whom ye were promised in the Books of God, the Holy, the Almighty, the All-Praised. How long will ye wander in the wilderness of heedlessness and superstition? Turn with your hearts in the direction of your Lord, the Forgiving, the Generous."

"Say: O concourse of monks! Seclude not yourselves 256 in churches and cloisters. Come forth by My leave, and occupy yourselves with that which will profit your souls and the souls of men. Thus biddeth you the King of the Day of Reckoning. Seclude yourselves in the stronghold of My love. This, verily, is a befitting seclusion, were ye of them that perceive it. He that shutteth himself up in a house is indeed as one dead. It behooveth man to show forth that which will profit all created things, and he that bringeth forth no fruit is fit for fire. Thus counseleth you your Lord, and He, verily, is the Almighty, the All-Bounteous. Enter ye into wedlock, that after you someone may fill your place. We have forbidden you perfidious acts, and not that which will demonstrate fidelity. Have ye clung to the standards fixed by your own selves, and cast the standards of God behind your backs? Fear God, and be not of the foolish. But for man, who would make mention of Me on My earth, and how could My attributes and My name *have been revealed? Ponder ye, and be not of them that are veiled and fast asleep. He that wedded not* [Jesus] *found no place wherein to dwell or lay His head, by reason of that which the hands of the treacherous had wrought. His sanctity consisteth not in that which ye believe or fancy, but rather in the things We possess. Ask, that ye may apprehend His station which hath been exalted above the imaginings of all that dwell on earth. Blessed are they who perceive it."* And again: *"O concourse of monks! If ye choose to follow Me, I will make you heirs of My Kingdom; and if ye transgress against Me, I will, in My longsuffering, endure it patiently, and I, verily, am the Ever-Forgiving, the All-Merciful. . . . Bethlehem is astir with the Breeze of God. We hear her voice saying: 'O Most Generous Lord! Where is Thy great glory established? The sweet savors of Thy presence have quickened me, after I had melted in my separation from Thee. Praised be Thou in that Thou hast raised the veils, and come with power in evident glory.' We called unto her from behind the Tabernacle of Majesty and Grandeur: 'O Bethlehem! This Light hath risen in the orient, and traveled towards the occident, until it reached thee in the evening of its life. Tell Me then: Do the sons recognize the Father, and acknowledge Him, or do they deny Him, even as the people aforetime denied Him* [Jesus]*?' Whereupon she cried out saying: 'Thou art, in truth, the All-Knowing, the Best-Informed.'"* And again: *"Consider, likewise, how numerous at this time are the monks who have secluded themselves in their churches, in My name, and who, when the appointed time came, and We unveiled to them Our beauty, failed to rec-*

ognize Me, notwithstanding that they call upon Me at dawn and at eventide." "Read ye the Evangel," He again addresses them, *"and yet refuse to acknowledge the All-Glorious Lord? This indeed beseemeth you not, O concourse of learned men! . . . The fragrances of the All-Merciful have wafted over all creation. Happy the man that hath forsaken his desires, and taken fast hold of guidance."*

These *"fallen stars"* of the firmament of Christendom, these *"thick clouds"* that have obscured the radiance of the true Faith of God, these princes of the Church that have failed to acknowledge the sovereignty of the *"King of kings,"* these deluded ministers of the Son who have shunned and ignored the promised Kingdom which the *"Everlasting Father"* has brought down from heaven, and is now establishing upon earth—these are experiencing, in this *"Day of Reckoning,"* a crisis, not indeed as critical as that which the Islamic sacerdotal order, the inveterate enemies of the Faith, has had to face, but one which is no less widespread and significant. *"Power hath been seized"* indeed, and is being increasingly seized, from these ecclesiastics that speak in the name, and yet are so far away from the spirit, of the Faith they profess. 257

We have only to look around us, as we survey the fortunes of Christian ecclesiastical orders, to appreciate the steady deterioration of their influence, the decline of their power, the damage to their prestige, the flouting of their authority, the dwindling of their congregations, the relaxation of their discipline, the re- 258 striction of their press, the timidity of their leaders, the confusion in their ranks, the progressive confiscation of their properties, the surrender of some of their most powerful strongholds, and the extinction of other ancient and cherished institutions. Indeed, ever since the Divine summons was issued, and the invitation extended, and the warning sounded, and the condemnation pronounced, this process, that may be said to have been initiated with the collapse of the temporal sovereignty of the Roman Pontiff, soon after the Tablet to the Pope had been revealed, has been operating with increasing momentum, menacing the very basis on which the entire order is resting. Aided by the forces which the Communist movement has unloosed, reinforced by the political consequences of the last war, accelerated by the excessive, the blind, the intolerant, and militant nationalism which is now convulsing the nations, and stimulated by the rising tide of materialism, irreligion, and paganism, this process is not only tending to subvert ecclesiastical institutions, but appears to be leading to the rapid dechristianization of the masses in many Christian countries.

259   I shall content myself with the enumeration of certain outstanding manifestations of this force which is increasingly invading the domain, and assailing the firmest ramparts, of one of the leading religious systems of mankind. The virtual extinction of the temporal power of the most preeminent ruler in Christendom immediately after the creation of the King-

dom of Italy; the wave of anticlericalism that swept over France after the collapse of the Napoleonic empire, and which culminated in the complete separation of the Catholic Church from the state, in the laicization of the Third Republic, in the secularization of education, and in the suppression and dispersal of religious orders; the swift and sudden rise of that "religious irreligion," that bold, conscious, and organized assault launched in Soviet Russia against the Greek Orthodox Church, that precipitated the disestablishment of the state religion, that massacred a vast number of its members originally numbering above a hundred million souls, that pulled down, closed, or converted into museums, theatres and warehouses, thousands upon thousands of churches, monasteries, synagogues and mosques, that stripped the church of its six and a half million acres of property, and sought, through its League of Militant Atheists and the promulgation of a "five-year plan of godlessness," to loosen from its foundations the religious life of the masses; the dismemberment of the Austro-Hungarian Monarchy that dissolved, by one stroke, the most powerful unit which owed its allegiance to, and supported through its resources the administration of, the Church of Rome; the divorce of the Spanish state from that same Church, and the overthrow of the monarchy, the champion of Catholic Christendom; the nationalistic philosophy, the parent of an unbridled and obsolete nationalism, which, having dethroned Islám, has in-

directly assaulted the front line of the Christian church
in non-Christian lands, and is dealing such heavy blows
to Catholic, Anglican, and Presbyterian Missions in
Persia, Turkey, and the Far East; the revolutionary
movement that brought in its wake the persecution of
the Catholic Church in Mexico; and finally the gospel
of modern paganism, unconcealed, aggressive, and
unrelenting, which, in the years preceding the present
turmoil, and increasingly since its outbreak, has swept
over the continent of Europe, invading the citadels,
and sowing confusion in the hearts of the supporters,
of the Catholic, the Greek Orthodox, and the Lutheran
churches, in Austria, Poland, the Baltic and Scandi-
navian states, and more recently in Western Europe,
the home and center of the most powerful hierarchies
of Christendom.

Christian Nations against
Christian Nations

260 What a sorry spectacle of impotence and disruption
does this fratricidal war, which Christian nations are
waging against Christian nations—Anglicans pitted
against Lutherans, Catholics against Greek Orthodox,
Catholics against Catholics, and Protestants against
Protestants—in support of a so-called Christian civilization, offer to the eyes of those who are already per-
ceiving the bankruptcy of the institutions that claim

to speak in the name, and to be the custodians, of the Faith of Jesus Christ! The powerlessness and despair of the Holy See to halt this internecine strife, in which the children of the Prince of Peace—blessed and supported by the benedictions and harangues of the prelates of a hopelessly divided church—are engaged, proclaim the degree of subservience into which the once all-powerful institutions of the Christian Faith have sunk, and are a striking reminder of the parallel state of decadence into which the hierarchies of its sister religion have fallen.

How tragically has Christendom ignored, and how 261 far it has strayed from, that high mission which He Who is the true Prince of Peace has, in these, the concluding passages of His Tablet to Pope Pius IX, called upon the entire body of Christians to fulfill—passages which establish, for all time, the distinction between the Mission of Bahá'u'lláh in this age and that of Jesus Christ: *"Say: O concourse of Christians! We have, on a previous occasion, revealed Ourself unto you, and ye recognized Me not. This is yet another occasion vouchsafed unto you. This is the Day of God; turn ye unto Him. . . . The Beloved One loveth not that ye be consumed with the fire of your desires. Were ye to be shut out as by a veil from Him, this would be for no other reason than your own waywardness and ignorance. Ye make mention of Me, and know Me not. Ye call upon Me, and are heedless of My Revelation. . . . O people of the Gospel! They who were not in the Kingdom have now entered it, whilst We be-*

hold you, in this day, tarrying at the gate. Rend the veils asunder by the power of your Lord, the Almighty, the All-Bounteous, and enter, then, in My name My Kingdom. Thus biddeth you He Who desireth for you everlasting life. . . . We behold you, O children of the Kingdom, in darkness. This, verily, beseemeth you not. Are ye, in the face of the Light, fearful because of your deeds? Direct yourselves towards Him. . . . Verily, He [Jesus] *said: 'Come ye after Me, and I will make you to become fishers of men.' In this day, however, We say: 'Come ye after Me, that We may make you to become the quickeners of mankind.'"* "Say," He moreover has written, *"We, verily, have come for your sakes, and have borne the misfortunes of the world for your salvation. Flee ye the One Who hath sacrificed His life that ye may be quickened? Fear God, O followers of the Spirit* [Jesus], *and walk not in the footsteps of every divine that hath gone far astray. . . . Open the doors of your hearts. He Who is the Spirit* [Jesus] *verily, standeth before them. Wherefore keep ye afar from Him Who hath purposed to draw you nigh unto a Resplendent Spot? Say: We, in truth, have opened unto you the gates of the Kingdom. Will ye bar the doors of your houses in My face? This indeed is naught but a grievous error."*

262　　Such is the pass to which the Christian clergy have come—a clergy that have interposed themselves between their flock and the Christ returned in the glory of the Father. As the Faith of this Promised One penetrates farther and farther into the heart of Christendom, as its recruits from the garrisons which its

spirit is assailing multiply, and provoke a concerted
and determined action in defense of the strongholds
of Christian orthodoxy, and as the forces of nationalism, paganism, secularism and racialism move jointly
towards a climax, might we not expect that the decline
in the power, the authority, and the prestige of these
ecclesiastics will be accentuated, and further demonstrate the truth, and more fully unfold the implications, of Bahá'u'lláh's pronouncement predicting the
eclipse of the luminaries of the Church of Jesus Christ.

Devastating indeed has been the havoc wrought 263
in the fortunes of the S͟hí'ih hierarchy in Persia, and
pitiable the lot reserved for its remnant now groaning
under the yoke of a civil authority it had for centuries
scorned and dominated. Cataclysmic indeed has been
the collapse of the most preeminent institution of Sunní
Islám, and irretrievable the downfall of its hierarchy
in a country that had championed the cause of the
self-styled vicar of the Prophet of God. Steady and
relentless is the process which has brought such destruction, shame, division, and weakness to the de-
fenders of the strongholds of Christian ecclesiasticism,
and black indeed are the clouds that darken its horizon. Through the actions of Muslim and Christian
divines— "idols," whom Bahá'u'lláh has stigmatized as
constituting the majority of His enemies—who failed,
as commanded by Him, to lay aside their pens and
fling away their fancies, and who, as He Himself testified, had they believed in Him would have brought

about the conversion of the masses, Islám and Christianity have, it would be no exaggeration to say, entered the most critical phase of their history.

264   Let none, however, mistake my purpose, or misrepresent this cardinal truth which is of the essence of the Faith of Bahá'u'lláh. The divine origin of all the Prophets of God—including Jesus Christ and the Apostle of God, the two greatest Manifestations preceding the Revelation of the Báb—is unreservedly and unshakably upheld by each and every follower of the Bahá'í religion. The fundamental unity of these Messengers of God is clearly recognized, the continuity of their Revelations is affirmed, the God-given authority and correlative character of their Books is admitted, the singleness of their aims and purposes is proclaimed, the uniqueness of their influence emphasized, the ultimate reconciliation of their teachings and followers taught and anticipated. *"They all,"* according to Bahá'u'lláh's testimony, *"abide in the same tabernacle, soar in the same heaven, are seated upon the same throne, utter the same speech, and proclaim the same Faith."*

The Continuity of Revelation

265 The Faith standing identified with the name of Bahá'u'lláh disclaims any intention to belittle any of the Prophets gone before Him, to whittle down any of their teachings, to obscure, however slightly, the radiance of their Revelations, to oust them from the hearts

of their followers, to abrogate the fundamentals of their
doctrines, to discard any of their revealed Books, or to
suppress the legitimate aspirations of their adherents.
Repudiating the claim of any religion to be the final
revelation of God to man, disclaiming finality for His
own Revelation, Bahá'u'lláh inculcates the basic principle of the relativity of religious truth, the continuity
of Divine Revelation, the progressiveness of religious
experience. His aim is to widen the basis of all revealed
religions and to unravel the mysteries of their scriptures. He insists on the unqualified recognition of the
unity of their purpose, restates the eternal verities they
enshrine, coordinates their functions, distinguishes the
essential and the authentic from the nonessential and
spurious in their teachings, separates the God-given
truths from the priest-prompted superstitions, and on
this as a basis proclaims the possibility, and even prophesies the inevitability, of their unification, and the consummation of their highest hopes.

As to Muḥammad, the Apostle of God, let none 266
among His followers who read these pages, think for a
moment that either Islám, or its Prophet, or His Book,
or His appointed Successors, or any of His authentic
teachings, have been, or are to be in any way, or to
however slight a degree, disparaged. The lineage of the
Báb, the descendant of the Imám Ḥusayn; the divers
and striking evidences, in Nabíl's Narrative, of the attitude of the Herald of our Faith towards the Founder,
the Imáms, and the Book of Islám; the glowing trib-
utes paid by Bahá'u'lláh in the Kitáb-i-Íqán to Mu-

ḥammad and His lawful Successors, and particularly
to the *"peerless and incomparable"* Imám Ḥusayn; the
arguments adduced, forcibly, fearlessly, and publicly
by 'Abdu'l-Bahá, in churches and synagogues, to demonstrate the validity of the Message of the Arabian
Prophet; and last but not least the written testimonial
of the Queen of Rumania, who, born in the Anglican
faith and notwithstanding the close alliance of her
government with the Greek Orthodox Church, the
state religion of her adopted country, has, largely as a
result of the perusal of these public discourses of
'Abdu'l-Bahá, been prompted to proclaim her recognition of the prophetic function of Muḥammad—all
proclaim, in no uncertain terms, the true attitude of
the Bahá'í Faith towards its parent religion.

267   "God," is her royal tribute, "is All, everything. He
is the power behind all beginnings. . . . His is the Voice
within us that shows us good and evil. But mostly we
ignore or misunderstand this voice. Therefore, did He
choose His Elect to come down amongst us upon earth
to make clear His Word, His real meaning. Therefore,
the Prophets; therefore, Christ, Muḥammad, Bahá'-
u'lláh, for man needs from time to time a voice upon
earth to bring God to him, to sharpen the realization
of the existence of the true God. Those voices sent to
us had to become flesh, so that with our earthly ears
we should be able to hear and understand."

268   What greater proof, it may be pertinently asked,
can the divines of either Persia or Turkey require wherewith to demonstrate the recognition by the followers

of Bahá'u'lláh of the exalted position occupied by the
Prophet Muḥammad among the entire company of
the Messengers of God? What greater service do these
divines expect us to render the Cause of Islám? What
greater evidence of our competence can they demand
than that we should kindle, in quarters so far beyond
their reach, the spark of an ardent and sincere conversion to the truth voiced by the Apostle of God, and
obtain from the pen of royalty this public, and indeed
historic, confession of His God-given Mission?

As to the position of Christianity, let it be stated   269
without any hesitation or equivocation that its divine
origin is unconditionally acknowledged, that the
Sonship and Divinity of Jesus Christ are fearlessly asserted, that the divine inspiration of the Gospel is fully
recognized, that the reality of the mystery of the Im-
maculacy of the Virgin Mary is confessed, and the
primacy of Peter, the Prince of the Apostles, is upheld
and defended. The Founder of the Christian Faith is
designated by Bahá'u'lláh as the *"Spirit of God,"* is proclaimed as the One Who *"appeared out of the breath of
the Holy Ghost,"* and is even extolled as the *"Essence of
the Spirit."* His mother is described as *"that veiled and
immortal, that most beauteous, countenance,"* and the
station of her Son eulogized as a *"station which hath
been exalted above the imaginings of all that dwell on
earth,"* whilst Peter is recognized as one whom God
has caused *"the mysteries of wisdom and of utterance to
flow out of his mouth."* *"Know thou,"* Bahá'u'lláh has
moreover testified, *"that when the Son of Man yielded*

up His breath to God, the whole creation wept with a great weeping. By sacrificing Himself, however, a fresh capacity was infused into all created things. Its evidences, as witnessed in all the peoples of the earth, are now manifest before thee. The deepest wisdom which the sages have uttered, the profoundest learning which any mind hath unfolded, the arts which the ablest hands have produced, the influence exerted by the most potent of rulers, are but manifestations of the quickening power released by His transcendent, His all-pervasive and resplendent Spirit. We testify that when He came into the world, He shed the splendor of His glory upon all created things. Through Him the leper recovered from the leprosy of perversity and ignorance. Through Him the unchaste and wayward were healed. Through His power, born of Almighty God, the eyes of the blind were opened and the soul of the sinner sanctified. . . . He it is Who purified the world. Blessed is the man who, with a face beaming with light, hath turned towards Him."

270   Indeed, the essential prerequisites of admittance into the Bahá'í fold of Jews, Zoroastrians, Hindus, Buddhists, and the followers of other ancient faiths, as well as of agnostics and even atheists, is the wholehearted and unqualified acceptance by them all of the divine origin of both Islám and Christianity, of the Prophetic functions of both Muḥammad and Jesus Christ, of the legitimacy of the institution of the Imamate, and of the primacy of St. Peter, the Prince of the Apostles. Such are the central, the solid, the incontrovertible principles that constitute the bedrock of Bahá'í

belief, which the Faith of Bahá'u'lláh is proud to acknowledge, which its teachers proclaim, which its apologists defend, which its literature disseminates, which its summer schools expound, and which the rank and file of its followers attest by both word and deed.

Nor should it be thought for a moment that the 271 followers of Bahá'u'lláh either seek to degrade or even belittle the rank of the world's religious leaders, whether Christian, Muslim, or of any other denomination, should their conduct conform to their professions, and be worthy of the position they occupy. *"Those divines,"* Bahá'u'lláh has affirmed, *". . . who are truly adorned with the ornament of knowledge and of a goodly character are, verily, as a head to the body of the world, and as eyes to the nations. The guidance of men hath, at all times, been and is dependent upon these blessed souls."* And again: *"The divine whose conduct is upright, and the sage who is just, are as the spirit unto the body of the world. Well is it with that divine whose head is attired with the crown of justice, and whose temple is adorned with the ornament of equity."* And yet again: *"The divine who hath seized and quaffed the most holy Wine, in the name of the sovereign Ordainer, is as an eye unto the world. Well is it with them who obey him, and call him to remembrance."* *"Great is the blessedness of that divine,"* He, in another connection, has written, *"that hath not allowed knowledge to become a veil between him and the One Who is the Object of all knowledge, and who, when the Self-Subsisting appeared, hath turned with a beaming face towards Him. He, in truth, is numbered with the learned.*

*The inmates of Paradise seek the blessing of his breath,
and his lamp sheddeth its radiance over all who are in
heaven and on earth. He, verily, is numbered with the
inheritors of the Prophets. He that beholdeth him hath,
verily, beheld the True One, and he that turneth towards
him hath, verily, turned towards God, the Almighty, the
All-Wise."* "*Respect ye the divines amongst you,*" is His
exhortation, "*them whose acts conform to the knowledge
they possess, who observe the statutes of God, and decree
the things God hath decreed in the Book. Know ye that
they are the lamps of guidance betwixt earth and heaven.
They that have no consideration for the position and merit
of the divines amongst them have, verily, altered the bounty
of God vouchsafed unto them.*"

272   Dear friends! I have, in the preceding pages, attempted to represent this world-afflicting ordeal that
has laid its grip upon mankind as primarily a judgment of God pronounced against the peoples of the
earth, who, for a century, have refused to recognize
the One Whose advent had been promised to all religions, and in Whose Faith all nations can alone, and
must eventually, seek their true salvation. I have quoted
certain passages from the writings of Bahá'u'lláh and
the Báb that reveal the character, and foreshadow the
occurrence of this divinely inflicted visitation. I have
enumerated the woeful trials with which the Faith, its
Herald, its Founder, and its Exemplar, have been
afflicted, and exposed the tragic failure of the general-

ity of mankind and its leaders to protest against these
tribulations, and to acknowledge the claims advanced
by those Who bore them. I have, moreover, indicated
that a direct, an awful, an inescapable responsibility
rested on the sovereigns of the earth and the world's
religious leaders who, in the days of the Báb and
Bahá'u'lláh, held within their grasp the reins of absolute political and religious authority. I have also en-
deavored to show how, as a result of the direct and
active antagonism of some of them to the Faith, and
the neglect by others of their unquestioned duty to
investigate its truth and its claims, to vindicate its in-
nocence, and avenge its injuries, both kings and ecclesiastics have been, and are still being, subjected to the
dire punishments which their sins of omission and
commission have provoked. I have, owing to the chief
responsibility which they incurred, as a result of the
undisputed ascendancy they held over their subjects
and followers, quoted extensively from the messages,
the exhortations and warnings addressed to them by
the Founders of our Faith, and expatiated on the consequences that have flowed from these momentous and
epoch-making utterances.

This great retributive calamity, for which the 273
world's supreme leaders, both secular and religious, are
to be regarded as primarily answerable, as testified by
Bahá'u'lláh, should not, if we would correctly appraise
it, be regarded solely as a punishment meted out by
God to a world that has, for a hundred years, persisted

in its refusal to embrace the truth of the redemptive
Message proffered to it by the supreme Messenger of
God in this day. It should be viewed also, though to a
lesser degree, in the light of a divine retribution for the
perversity of the human race in general, in casting itself adrift from those elementary principles which must,
at all times, govern, and can alone safeguard, the life
and progress of mankind. Humanity has, alas, with
increasing insistence, preferred, instead of acknowledg-
ing and adoring the Spirit of God as embodied in His
religion in this day, to worship those false idols, un-
truths and half-truths, which are obscuring its religions,
corrupting its spiritual life, convulsing its political institutions, corroding its social fabric, and shattering
its economic structure.

274   Not only have the peoples of the earth ignored,
and some of them even assailed, a Faith which is at
once the essence, the promise, the reconciler, and the
unifier of all religions, but they have drifted away from
their own religions, and set up on their subverted altars other gods wholly alien not only to the spirit but
to the traditional forms of their ancient faiths.

275   *"The face of the world,"* Bahá'u'lláh laments, *"hath
altered. The way of God and the religion of God have
ceased to be of any worth in the eyes of men." "The vitality
of men's belief in God,"* He also has written, *"is dying out
in every land. . . . The corrosion of ungodliness is eating
into the vitals of human society." "Religion,"* He affirms,
"is verily the chief instrument for the establishment of or-

*der in the world, and of tranquility amongst its peoples.
. . . The greater the decline of religion, the more grievous
the waywardness of the ungodly. This cannot but lead in
the end to chaos and confusion."* And again: *"Religion is a
radiant light and an impregnable stronghold for the protection and welfare of the peoples of the world." "As the
body of man,"* He, in another connection, has written,
*"needeth a garment to clothe it, so the body of mankind
must needs be adorned with the mantle of justice and
wisdom. Its robe is the Revelation vouchsafed unto it by
God."*

The Three False Gods

This vital force is dying out, this mighty agency has 276
been scorned, this radiant light obscured, this impregnable stronghold abandoned, this beauteous robe dis-
carded. God Himself has indeed been dethroned from
the hearts of men, and an idolatrous world passionately and clamorously hails and worships the false gods
which its own idle fancies have fatuously created, and
its misguided hands so impiously exalted. The chief
idols in the desecrated temple of mankind are none
other than the triple gods of Nationalism, Racialism
and Communism, at whose altars governments and
peoples, whether democratic or totalitarian, at peace
or at war, of the East or of the West, Christian or Islamic, are, in various forms and in different degrees,

now worshiping. Their high priests are the politicians and the worldly-wise, the so-called sages of the age; their sacrifice, the flesh and blood of the slaughtered multitudes; their incantations, outworn shibboleths and insidious and irreverent formulas; their incense, the smoke of anguish that ascends from the lacerated hearts of the bereaved, the maimed, and the homeless.

277   The theories and policies, so unsound, so pernicious, which deify the state and exalt the nation above mankind, which seek to subordinate the sister races of the world to one single race, which discriminate between the black and the white, and which tolerate the dominance of one privileged class over all others—these are the dark, the false, and crooked doctrines for which any man or people who believes in them, or acts upon them, must, sooner or later, incur the wrath and chastisement of God.

278   *"Movements,"* is the warning sounded by 'Abdu'l-Bahá, *"newly born and worldwide in their range, will exert their utmost effort for the advancement of their designs. The Movement of the Left will acquire great importance. Its influence will spread."*

279   Contrasting with, and irreconcilably opposed to, these war-engendering, world-convulsing doctrines are the healing, the saving, the pregnant truths proclaimed by Bahá'u'lláh, the Divine Organizer and Savior of the whole human race—truths which should be regarded as the animating force and the hallmark of His Revelation: *"The world is but one country, and mankind its citizens."* *"Let not a man glory in that he loves his country;*

let him rather glory in this, that he loves his kind." And again: *"Ye are the fruits of one tree, and the leaves of one branch." "Bend your minds and wills to the education of the peoples and kindreds of the earth, that haply . . . all mankind may become the upholders of one order, and the inhabitants of one city. . . . Ye dwell in one world, and have been created through the operation of one Will." "Beware lest the desires of the flesh and of a corrupt inclination provoke divisions among you. Be ye as the fingers of one hand, the members of one body."* And yet again: *"All the saplings of the world have appeared from one Tree, and all the drops from one Ocean, and all beings owe their existence to one Being."* And furthermore: *"That one indeed is a man who today dedicateth himself to the service of the entire human race."*

The Weakened Pillars of Religion

Not only must irreligion and its monstrous offspring, the triple curse that oppresses the soul of mankind in this day, be held responsible for the ills which are so tragically besetting it, but other evils and vices, which are, for the most part, the direct consequences of the *"weakening of the pillars of religion,"* must also be regarded as contributory factors to the manifold guilt of which individuals and nations stand convicted. The signs of moral downfall, consequent to the dethronement of religion and the enthronement of these usurping idols, are too numerous and too patent for even a superficial observer of the state of present-day society to fail to notice. The spread of lawlessness, of drunkenness, of gambling, and of crime; the inordinate love of pleasure, of riches, and other earthly vanities; the laxity in morals, revealing itself in the irresponsible attitude towards marriage, in the weakening of parental control, in the rising tide of divorce, in the deterioration in the standard of literature and of the press, and in the advocacy of theories that are the very negation of purity, of morality and chastity—these evidences of moral decadence, invading both the East and the West, permeating every stratum of society, and instilling their poison in its members of both sexes, young and old alike, blacken still further the scroll upon which are inscribed the manifold transgressions of an unrepentant humanity.

281   Small wonder that Bahá'u'lláh, the Divine Physician, should have declared: *"In this day the tastes of men have changed, and their power of perception hath altered. The contrary winds of the world, and its colors, have provoked a cold, and deprived men's nostrils of the sweet savors of Revelation."*

282   Brimful and bitter indeed is the cup of humanity that has failed to respond to the summons of God as voiced by His Supreme Messenger, that has dimmed the lamp of its faith in its Creator, that has transferred, in so great a measure, the allegiance owed Him to the gods of its own invention, and polluted itself with the evils and vices which such a transference must necessarily engender.

Dear friends! It is in this light that we, the follow- 283
ers of Bahá'u'lláh, should regard this visitation of God
which, in the concluding years of the first century of
the Bahá'í era, afflicts the generality, and has thrown
into such a bewildering confusion the affairs, of mankind. It is because of this dual guilt, the things it has
done and the things it has left undone, its misdeeds as
well as its dismal and signal failure to accomplish its
clear and unmistakable duty towards God, His Messenger, and His Faith, that this grievous ordeal, whatever its immediate political and economic causes, has
laid its adamantine grip upon it.

God, however, as has been pointed out in the very 284
beginning of these pages, does not only punish the
wrongdoings of His children. He chastises because he
is just, and He chastens because He loves. Having chas-
tened them, He cannot, in His great mercy, leave them
to their fate. Indeed, by the very act of chastening them
He prepares them for the mission for which He has
created them. *"My calamity is My providence,"* He, by
the mouth of Bahá'u'lláh, has assured them, *"outwardly
it is fire and vengeance, but inwardly it is light and mercy."*

The flames which His Divine justice have kindled 285
cleanse an unregenerate humanity, and fuse its discor-
dant, its warring elements as no other agency can
cleanse or fuse them. It is not only a retributory and
destructive fire, but a disciplinary and creative process, whose aim is the salvation, through unification,
of the entire planet. Mysteriously, slowly, and resistlessly God accomplishes His design, though the sight

that meets our eyes in this day be the spectacle of a world hopelessly entangled in its own meshes, utterly careless of the Voice which, for a century, has been calling it to God, and miserably subservient to the siren voices which are attempting to lure it into the vast abyss.

God's Purpose

286 God's purpose is none other than to usher in, in ways He alone can bring about, and the full significance of which He alone can fathom, the Great, the Golden Age of a long-divided, a long-afflicted humanity. Its present state, indeed even its immediate future, is dark, distressingly dark. Its distant future, however, is radiant, gloriously radiant—so radiant that no eye can visualize it.

287 *"The winds of despair,"* writes Bahá'u'lláh, as He surveys the immediate destinies of mankind, *"are, alas, blowing from every direction, and the strife that divides and afflicts the human race is daily increasing. The signs of impending convulsions and chaos can now be discerned, inasmuch as the prevailing order appears to be lamentably defective."* *"Such shall be its plight,"* He, in another connection, has declared, *"that to disclose it now would not be meet and seemly."* *"These fruitless strifes,"* He, on the other hand, contemplating the future of mankind, has emphatically prophesied, in the course of His memorable interview with the Persian orientalist, Ed-

ward G. Browne, *"these ruinous wars shall pass away, and the 'Most Great Peace' shall come. . . . These strifes and this bloodshed and discord must cease, and all men be as one kindred and one family."* *"Soon,"* He predicts, *"will the present-day order be rolled up, and a new one spread out in its stead."* *"After a time,"* He also has written, *"all the governments on earth will change. Oppression will envelop the world. And following a universal convulsion, the sun of justice will rise from the horizon of the unseen realm."* *"The whole earth,"* He, moreover, has stated, *"is now in a state of pregnancy. The day is approaching when it will have yielded its noblest fruits, when from it will have sprung forth the loftiest trees, the most enchanting blossoms, the most heavenly blessings."* *"All nations and kindreds,"* 'Abdu'l-Bahá likewise has written, *". . . will become a single nation. Religious and sectarian antagonism, the hostility of races and peoples, and differences among nations, will be eliminated. All men will adhere to one religion, will have one common faith, will be blended into one race, and become a single people. All will dwell in one common fatherland, which is the planet itself."*

What we witness at the present time, during "this gravest crisis in the history of civilization," recalling such times in which "religions have perished and are born," is the adolescent stage in the slow and painful evolution of humanity, preparatory to the attainment of the stage of manhood, the stage of maturity, the promise of which is embedded in the teachings, and enshrined in the prophecies, of Bahá'u'lláh. The tumult of this age of transition is characteristic of the impetuosity and irrational instincts of youth, its follies, its prodigality, its pride, its self-assurance, its rebelliousness, and contempt of discipline.

The Great Age to Come

289 The ages of its infancy and childhood are past, never again to return, while the Great Age, the consummation of all ages, which must signalize the coming of age of the entire human race, is yet to come. The convulsions of this transitional and most turbulent period in the annals of humanity are the essential prerequisites, and herald the inevitable approach, of that Age of Ages, *"the time of the end,"* in which the folly and tumult of strife that has, since the dawn of history, blackened the annals of mankind, will have been finally transmuted into the wisdom and the tranquility of an undisturbed, a universal, and lasting peace, in which the discord and separation of the children of men will have given way to the worldwide reconciliation, and the complete unification of the divers elements that constitute human society.

290 This will indeed be the fitting climax of that process of integration which, starting with the family, the smallest unit in the scale of human organization, must, after having called successively into being the tribe, the city-state, and the nation, continue to operate until

it culminates in the unification of the whole world, the final object and the crowning glory of human evolution on this planet. It is this stage which humanity, willingly or unwillingly, is resistlessly approaching. It is for this stage that this vast, this fiery ordeal which humanity is experiencing is mysteriously paving the way. It is with this stage that the fortunes and the purpose of the Faith of Bahá'u'lláh are indissolubly linked. It is the creative energies which His Revelation has released in the *"year sixty,"* and later reinforced by the successive effusions of celestial power vouchsafed in the *"year nine"* and the *"year eighty"* to all mankind, that have instilled into humanity the capacity to attain this final stage in its organic and collective evolution. It is with the Golden Age of His Dispensation that the consummation of this process will be forever associated. It is the structure of His New World Order, now stirring in the womb of the administrative institutions He Himself has created, that will serve both as a pattern and a nucleus of that world commonwealth which is the sure, the inevitable destiny of the peoples and nations of the earth.

Just as the organic evolution of mankind has been 291 slow and gradual, and involved successively the unification of the family, the tribe, the city-state, and the nation, so has the light vouchsafed by the Revelation of God, at various stages in the evolution of religion, and reflected in the successive Dispensations of the past, been slow and progressive. Indeed the measure of Divine Revelation, in every age, has been adapted to, and commensurate with, the degree of social progress achieved in that age by a constantly evolving humanity.

292   *"It hath been decreed by Us,"* explains Bahá'u'lláh, *"that the Word of God, and all the potentialities thereof, shall be manifested unto men in strict conformity with such conditions as have been foreordained by Him Who is the All-Knowing, the All-Wise. . . . Should the Word be allowed to release suddenly all the energies latent within it, no man could sustain the weight of so mighty a Revelation." "All created things,"* 'Abdu'l-Bahá, elucidating this truth, has affirmed, *"have their degree or stage of maturity. The period of maturity in the life of a tree is the time of its fruit-bearing. . . . The animal attains a stage of full growth and completeness, and in the human kingdom man reaches his maturity when the light of his intelligence attains its greatest power and development. . . . Similarly there are periods and stages in the collective life of humanity. At one time it was passing through its stage of childhood, at another its period of youth, but now it has entered its long-predicted phase of maturity, the evidences of which are everywhere apparent. . . . That which was applicable to human needs during the early history of the race can neither meet nor satisfy the demands of this day, this period of newness and consummation. Humanity has emerged from its former state of limitation and preliminary training. Man must now become imbued with new virtues and powers, new moral standards, new ca-*

pacities. New bounties, perfect bestowals, are awaiting and already descending upon him. The gifts and blessings of the period of youth, although timely and sufficient during the adolescence of mankind, are now incapable of meeting the requirements of its maturity." "In every Dispensation," He moreover has written, *"the light of Divine Guidance has been focused upon one central theme. . . . In this wondrous Revelation, this glorious century, the foundation of the Faith of God, and the distinguishing feature of His Law, is the consciousness of the oneness of mankind."*

Religion and Social Evolution

The Revelation associated with the Faith of Jesus Christ   293
focused attention primarily on the redemption of the individual and the molding of his conduct, and stressed, as its central theme, the necessity of inculcating a high standard of morality and discipline into man, as the fundamental unit in human society. Nowhere in the Gospels do we find any reference to the unity of nations or the unification of mankind as a whole. When Jesus spoke to those around Him, He addressed them primarily as individuals rather than as component parts of one universal, indivisible entity. The whole surface of the earth was as yet unexplored, and the organization of all its peoples and nations as one unit could, consequently, not be envisaged, how much less pro-

claimed or established. What other interpretation can be given to these words, addressed specifically by Bahá'u'lláh to the followers of the Gospel, in which the fundamental distinction between the Mission of Jesus Christ, concerning primarily the individual, and His own Message, directed more particularly to mankind as a whole, has been definitely established: *"Verily, He* [Jesus] *said: 'Come ye after Me, and I will make you to become fishers of men.' In this day, however, We say: 'Come ye after Me, that We may make you to become the quickeners of mankind.'"*

294   The Faith of Islám, the succeeding link in the chain of Divine Revelation, introduced, as Bahá'u'lláh Himself testifies, the conception of the nation as a unit and a vital stage in the organization of human society, and embodied it in its teaching. This indeed is what is meant by this brief yet highly significant and illuminating pronouncement of Bahá'u'lláh: *"Of old* [Islamic Dispensation] *it hath been revealed: 'Love of one's country is an element of the Faith of God.'"* This principle was established and stressed by the Apostle of God, inasmuch as the evolution of human society required it at that time. Nor could any stage above and beyond it have been envisaged, as world conditions preliminary to the establishment of a superior form of organization were as yet unobtainable. The conception of nationality, the attainment to the state of nationhood, may, therefore, be said to be the distinguishing characteristics of the Muḥammadan Dispensation, in the course of which the nations and races of the world,

and particularly in Europe and America, were unified and achieved political independence.

'Abdu'l-Bahá Himself elucidates this truth in one 295 of His Tablets: *"In cycles gone by, though harmony was established, yet, owing to the absence of means, the unity of all mankind could not have been achieved. Continents remained widely divided, nay even among the peoples of one and the same continent association and interchange of thought were well-nigh impossible. Consequently intercourse, understanding and unity amongst all the peoples and kindreds of the earth were unattainable. In this day, however, means of communication have multiplied, and the five continents of the earth have virtually merged into one. . . . In like manner all the members of the human family, whether peoples or governments, cities or villages, have become increasingly interdependent. For none is self-sufficiency any longer possible, inasmuch as political ties unite all peoples and nations, and the bonds of trade and industry, of agriculture and education, are being strengthened every day. Hence the unity of all mankind can in this day be achieved. Verily this is none other but one of the wonders of this wondrous age, this glorious century. Of this past ages have been deprived, for this century— the century of light—has been endowed with unique and unprecedented glory, power and illumination. Hence the miraculous unfolding of a fresh marvel every day. Eventually it will be seen how bright its candles will burn in the assemblage of man."*

"Behold," He further explains, *"how its light is now* 296 *dawning upon the world's darkened horizon. The first*

candle is unity in the political realm, the early glimmerings of which can now be discerned. The second candle is unity of thought in world undertakings, the consummation of which will erelong be witnessed. The third candle is unity in freedom which will surely come to pass. The fourth candle is unity in religion which is the cornerstone of the foundation itself, and which, by the power of God, will be revealed in all its splendor. The fifth candle is the unity of nations—a unity which, in this century, will be securely established, causing all the peoples of the world to regard themselves as citizens of one common fatherland. The sixth candle is unity of races, making of all that dwell on earth peoples and kindreds of one race. The seventh candle is unity of language, i.e., the choice of a universal tongue in which all peoples will be instructed and converse. Each and every one of these will inevitably come to pass, inasmuch as the power of the Kingdom of God will aid and assist in their realization."

297   "One of the great events," 'Abdu'l-Bahá has, in His "Some Answered Questions," affirmed, "which is to occur in the Day of the manifestation of that Incomparable Branch [Bahá'u'lláh] is the hoisting of the Standard of God among all nations. By this is meant that all nations and kindreds will be gathered together under the shadow of this Divine Banner, which is no other than the Lordly Branch itself, and will become a single nation. Religious and sectarian antagonism, the hostility of races and peoples, and differences among nations, will be eliminated. All men will adhere to one religion, will have one

*common faith, will be blended into one race, and become
a single people. All will dwell in one common fatherland,
which is the planet itself."*

This is the stage which the world is now approach-   298
ing, the stage of world unity, which, as 'Abdu'l-Bahá
assures us, will, in this century, be securely established.
"The Tongue of Grandeur," Bahá'u'lláh Himself affirms,
*"hath . . . in the Day of His Manifestation proclaimed:
'It is not his to boast who loveth his country, but it is his
who loveth the world.'"* *"Through the power,"* He adds,
*"released by these exalted words He hath lent a fresh im-
pulse, and set a new direction, to the birds of men's hearts,
and hath obliterated every trace of restriction and limitation from God's Holy Book."*

The Wider, Inclusive Loyalty

A word of warning should, however, be uttered in this   299
connection. The love of one's country, instilled and
stressed by the teaching of Islám, as *"an element of the
Faith of God,"* has not, through this declaration, this
clarion-call of Bahá'u'lláh, been either condemned or
disparaged. It should not, indeed it cannot, be construed as a repudiation, or regarded in the light of a
censure, pronounced against a sane and intelligent
patriotism, nor does it seek to undermine the allegiance
and loyalty of any individual to his country, nor does
it conflict with the legitimate aspirations, rights, and

duties of any individual state or nation. All it does imply and proclaim is the insufficiency of patriotism, in view of the fundamental changes effected in the economic life of society and the interdependence of the nations, and as the consequence of the contraction of the world, through the revolution in the means of transportation and communication—conditions that did not and could not exist either in the days of Jesus Christ or of Muḥammad. It calls for a wider loyalty, which should not, and indeed does not, conflict with lesser loyalties. It instills a love which, in view of its scope, must include and not exclude the love of one's own country. It lays, through this loyalty which it inspires, and this love which it infuses, the only foundation on which the concept of world citizenship can thrive, and the structure of world unification can rest. It does insist, however, on the subordination of national considerations and particularistic interests to the imperative and paramount claims of humanity as a whole, inasmuch as in a world of interdependent nations and peoples the advantage of the part is best to be reached by the advantage of the whole.

300   The world is, in truth, moving on towards its destiny. The interdependence of the peoples and nations of the earth, whatever the leaders of the divisive forces of the world may say or do, is already an accomplished fact. Its unity in the economic sphere is now understood and recognized. The welfare of the part means the welfare of the whole, and the distress of the part

brings distress to the whole. The Revelation of Bahá'u'lláh has, in His own words, *"lent a fresh impulse and set a new direction"* to this vast process now operating in the world. The fires lit by this great ordeal are the consequences of men's failure to recognize it. They are, moreover, hastening its consummation. Adversity, prolonged, worldwide, afflictive, allied to chaos and universal destruction, must needs convulse the nations, stir the conscience of the world, disillusion the masses, precipitate a radical change in the very conception of society, and coalesce ultimately the disjointed, the bleeding limbs of mankind into one body, single, organically united, and indivisible.

World Commonwealth

To the general character, the implications and features 301 of this world commonwealth, destined to emerge, sooner or later, out of the carnage, agony, and havoc of this great world convulsion, I have already referred in my previous communications. Suffice it to say that this consummation will, by its very nature, be a gradual process, and must, as Bahá'u'lláh has Himself anticipated, lead at first to the establishment of that Lesser Peace which the nations of the earth, as yet unconscious of His Revelation and yet unwittingly enforcing the general principles which He has enunciated, will themselves establish. This momentous and historic step, involving the reconstruction of mankind, as the result of the universal recognition of its oneness and wholeness, will bring in its wake the spiritualization of the masses, consequent to the recognition of the character, and the acknowledgment of the claims, of the Faith of Bahá'u'lláh—the essential condition to that ultimate fusion of all races, creeds, classes, and nations which must signalize the emergence of His New World Order.

302   Then will the coming of age of the entire human race be proclaimed and celebrated by all the peoples and nations of the earth. Then will the banner of the Most Great Peace be hoisted. Then will the worldwide sovereignty of Bahá'u'lláh—the Establisher of the Kingdom of the Father foretold by the Son, and anticipated by the Prophets of God before Him and after Him—be recognized, acclaimed, and firmly established. Then will a world civilization be born, flourish, and perpetuate itself, a civilization with a fullness of life such as the world has never seen nor can as yet conceive. Then will the Everlasting Covenant be fulfilled in its completeness. Then will the promise enshrined in all the Books of God be redeemed, and all the prophecies uttered by the Prophets of old come to pass, and the vision of seers and poets be realized. Then will the planet, galvanized through the universal belief of its dwellers in one God, and their allegiance to one common Revelation, mirror, within the limitations imposed upon it, the effulgent glories of the sov-

ereignty of Bahá'u'lláh, shining in the plenitude of its splendor in the Abhá Paradise, and be made the footstool of His Throne on high, and acclaimed as the earthly heaven, capable of fulfilling that ineffable destiny fixed for it, from time immemorial, by the love and wisdom of its Creator.

Not ours, puny mortals that we are, to attempt, at 303 so critical a stage in the long and checkered history of mankind, to arrive at a precise and satisfactory understanding of the steps which must successively lead a bleeding humanity, wretchedly oblivious of its God, and careless of Bahá'u'lláh, from its calvary to its ultimate resurrection. Not ours, the living witnesses of the all-subduing potency of His Faith, to question, for a moment, and however dark the misery that enshrouds the world, the ability of Bahá'u'lláh to forge, with the hammer of His Will, and through the fire of tribulation, upon the anvil of this travailing age, and in the particular shape His mind has envisioned, these scattered and mutually destructive fragments into which a perverse world has fallen, into one single unit, solid and indivisible, able to execute His design for the children of men.

Ours rather the duty, however confused the scene, 304 however dismal the present outlook, however circumscribed the resources we dispose of, to labor serenely, confidently, and unremittingly to lend our share of assistance, in whichever way circumstances may enable us, to the operation of the forces which, as marshaled and directed by Bahá'u'lláh, are leading humanity out of the valley of misery and shame to the loftiest summits of power and glory.

Shoghi

To the beloved of God and the handmaids of the Merciful throughout the West.

Haifa, Palestine
March 28, 1941

INDEX

*References to the words of Shoghi Effendi are indexed by paragraph number.
References to explanatory material not written by Shoghi Effendi are indexed
by page number and preceded by the abbreviation "p."*